How to Make $1,000 a Minute:
Negotiating Salaries & Raises

How to Make $1,000 a Minute: Negotiating Salaries & Raises

BY JACK CHAPMAN

President, Chicago Office, Bernard Haldane Associates
President, Professional Career Counselors & Consultants Network

TEN SPEED PRESS

Berkeley, California

Jack welcomes comments and questions about this book, career consulting
work, or the Professional Career Counselors & Consultants Network
(PCCN). Write to Jack Chapman, 511 Maple, Wilmette, IL 60091 or call
(312) 346-5835.

1🖘
TEN SPEED PRESS
P O Box 7123
Berkeley, California 94707

Book Design by Hal Hershey
Cover Design by Fifth Street Design
Illustrations by Fuzzy Randall

Library of Congress Cataloging in Publication Data

Chapman, Jack, 1945-
    How to make $1000 a minute.
        1. Promotions. 2. Wages. 3. Negotiation in business.
    4. Interpersonal relations. I. Title. II. Title: How to make one thousand
    dollars a minute.
HF5549.5.P7C48   1987   650.1'4   86-23099

ISBN: 0-89815-191-0

Printed in the United States of America

2   3   4   5   6   —   95   94   93   92   91

To all the clients, students, and friends
whose careers make my career possible,
thank you.
I have learned my craft from you.

Contents

Million Dollar Blunders

Calculating the Dollars You Can Make, or Lose, in Those Sixty Seconds of Negotiations □ Million Dollar Blunders □ Example 1: Mr. Eager Loses the Offer □ Example 2: Ms. Polite Loses $2,500 a Year □ Example 3: Mr. Hardwork Loses His Raise □ The Principle of Quality □ The Difference Between Vicious and Virtuous Cycles

Aiming for What You're Worth

Labor Is Intangible □ Salary Relates to Level of Responsibility □ The Universal Hiring Principle Is "Make Me a Buck" □ Million Dollar Blunders □ Example 4: Mr. Greedy Gets What He Deserves □ The Basic Principle of Effective Salary Negotiations

Salary-Making Rule 1: When to Discuss It

Ever Bought Something You Couldn't Afford? □ Waiting for the Right Moment □ How to Postpone Salary Talk: Part I □ What if They Get Mad at Me? □ Development of an Offer □ Seller/Buyer Role Reversal in Negotiations

ACKNOWLEDGEMENTS

I especially want to thank the following individuals for helping me create this book:

Karla Kizzort, who first invented my class "A Streetwise Guide to Job Interviewing." I developed much of this volume from teaching that course.

Marti Beddoe, Robin Sheerer, Nancy Ebaugh, and **Tom Camden**, who have been this career consultant's career consultants and who gave me support and suggestions about the book.

Armine Del Carmen who deserves a certificate in cryptography for deciphering all my scribbles, notes, and arrows for the second edition updates and expansions.

Mary Vallely, who handled the day-to-day logistics of a project that always required Step 2 to be finished before proceeding with Step 1.

Chuck Sterbis, my colleague and mentor in career consulting, who offered strategic criticism about the methods presented here, and **Judith Votel** and **Carol Semrad** who helped me clarify the "recruiters" section.

Tony Byrnes, who first nudged me to stop *thinking* about this book and *do* it.

And most important: **Karen**, my wife, whose vision encouraged me to go for it, and whose practical love and support made it possible.

Introduction

by Richard Germann*
author of *Job and Career Building*

Is it true that you can negotiate anything? The short answer is, "Of course you can!" But will it do you any good? This requires a longer answer. In my experience over the past twenty years, people who are facing negotiations can be divided roughly into three equal categories: those who don't try negotiating because they feel uncomfortable, don't know how, or have made up their minds it won't work; those who negotiate without plan or purpose and to no effect; and those who see negotiating as a valuable skill to develop and practice consciously.

The purpose of this book is to make significant inroads into those first two categories by spelling out purposes, principles, and specific techniques to help you develop and apply negotiating skills where they will do the most good.

The time you spend in becoming a skilled negotiator will probably be a 10 on the scale of good investments, when you consider the return in dollars alone. Beyond the financial rewards, though, are many benefits in terms of job satisfaction, interpersonal relationships, and career advancement. Often when agreement has been reached after vigorous negotiations, the clouds disappear, the sun comes out, and mutual respect between the negotiating parties translates into a solid and constructive future work relationship.

There are some conditions, however, that have to be satisfied for a mutually profitable outcome to be achieved. The first of these conditions is an understanding on your part of the situation in which you find yourself. Negotiating from ignorance is no better than negotiating from

Richard Germann is V.P. of Counselor and Product Development for Right Associates, an international career transition consulting firm headquartered in Philadelphia. He is the author of *Job and Career Building*, and *Working and Liking It.*

weakness. The early chapters of this book show you how to be aware of the purposes and hidden agendas of all the players involved, as well as the correct time to make your move.

The second, equally important, condition is the existence of a communications link between the parties. If you have and express a sincere concern for the other person's interests, you will have taken the first step toward establishing the rapport necessary for motivating him or her to respond positively to your negotiating initiatives. Consider the difference between the following statements:

I don't care about your problems; I need more money. . . .

I care about your company and its goals, and I want to help you achieve them. Here are some of the contributions I have made (or intend to make). . . .

The first statement will effectively close the other person's ears and mind; the second statement will engage the other person's interest in a positive way. Such a statement does not make your negotiating position a soft one. It simply establishes a positive climate for firm and purposeful negotiations with regard to either the starting salary for a new job or a salary increase for your current job.

The third condition for successful negotiations is a prepared strategy. You must have a clear purpose in mind before you begin to negotiate. Entering negotiations in the hope that you will achieve something — anything — as time passes, and that your purpose will become clear after you've heard the other person's point of view, is not only a recipe for failure but also the surest way to lose the person's respect.

This book will not only help you map out a clear purpose and understand the principles on which it must be based, but also supply the actual words you will use to articulate your purpose.

One more point about successful negotiating: Just as there are intelligent reasons for accepting (after due consideration) compromises in some areas, there are good reasons not to compromise in others. In any case both sides must win, or both will have to lose. In a win-lose situation, the resulting resentment, guilt, and loss of respect usually lead to long-term deterioration in human relationships.

To summarize: When entering into negotiations, know the situation. Understand the conditions and the points of view of the parties involved. Pinpoint the correct timing for starting the negotiation process to avoid becoming trapped in an unfavorable interchange. Decide what you want to accomplish and prepare your strategy, right down to rehearsing the actual words you're going to use. Create a favorable climate by stating your awareness of the other person's concerns, and then be firm, with limited flexibility, in following through to a mutually beneficial outcome.

This book contains tested, practical methodology rather than psychological theory. You can get immediate results from studying and practicing these techniques. By developing constructive negotiating habits over a period of time, you will also be able to manage any negotiating situation in the future and bring it to a successful conclusion.

PREFACE TO THE SECOND EDITION

Thank you to the many hundreds of readers who have called me with your salary stories! I have enjoyed talking with you and coaching you to more money. Your feedback has prompted me to make the following revisions.

1) You were so enthusiastic about the great results you got from my salary telecoaching service that I have expanded and highlighted that section in Chapter 11 with stories. New readers are encouraged to profit too — give me a call!

2) The pay comparison analysis service referenced in the first edition went out of business; I retained a nostalgic sample of a pay comparison and a plea for any entrepreneurial type to make me a proposal about how we could provide that service to the public with quality.

3) Some folks had a hard time finding diplomatic ways to postpone salary talk, so I added a new section in Chapter 3 called "What If They Get Mad At Me?"

4) I expanded the benefits and perquisites negotiation list and summarized it as a checklist in Figure 7-1 for you.

5) Salary-making Rule 5 is expressed differently, but it's the same rule. Salary-making Rule 5 used to read "Accept the Offer, Not the Job."

This edition emphasizes how positive and enthusiastic you should be. The rule now reads "Clinch the Deal and Deal Some More."

6) I have expanded the sales compensation section in Chapter 7 to define the terms and principles involved in draws, advances, and straight commission.

CHAPTER ONE

Million Dollar Blunders

Calculating the Dollars You Can Make, or Lose, in Those Sixty Seconds of Negotiations

We spend years planning what we'll be when we grow up. We put thousands of dollars and hours into school to get a degree and then spend weeks on resumes, letters, and ads. We schlepp from city to suburbs to city, talking to jerks, jokes, and gentlemen about their job openings. We put hours of practice into our sales pitch; hours of research into understanding the company; and two or three nervous days into interviews, straining to beat out the competition. The most important part, the whole reason we started in the first place—**Getting Paid**—we often handle in sixty seconds or less!

Then for months we roll up our sleeves, giving our new job every ounce of brains and drive we can supply. But when it's time for a raise, most of us just accept whatever we're offered. How many minutes do we spend discussing the money? Zero.

To negotiate either a salary or a raise, however, sixty seconds is all you'll need. You'll learn in this book how to make those sixty seconds count. You'll learn how to make thousands of dollars in those minutes, and improve your whole sense of work and worth.

Think a moment how that adds up.

A conservative estimate of an average lifetime wage, beginning at $10,000 a year and ending at $50,000, is $25,000 a year. Over forty-five years that totals $1,125,000! Even a simple 10-percent raise means an extra $112,500. You could buy your home with just a 10-percent raise.

Proper negotiations can *double* your income. Mishandling negotiations can be a Million Dollar Blunder.

And it's easy to blunder. In my many years as a career consultant, I've seen people earning only half their value just because they never asked for more "the right way." How would *you* handle these three situations?

Million Dollar Blunders

Example 1: Mr. Eager Loses the Offer

Mr. Eager is bright, ambitious, and interested in working hard. He expects to be paid fairly and at the top of his range. His potential employer is looking at Eager's record: The resume looks good; Eager has just the kind of experience the company could use and some solid examples of making things work right.

Anxious that he not waste his time, Eager pops the question in the most tactful way he can: "Well, let's see if we're in the right ballpark. I'm looking for a salary in the mid-forties."

Employer figures that's okay, but is just a touch put off. He thinks Eager should primarily be interested in long-term work with the company. This sounds like Eager's more interested in the money. Well, that's understandable, but Employer is also interviewing Mr. Dedicated for the job. While he doesn't know what Dedicated's price range is, it sure sounds like *he's* interested in the company. "After all," Employer decides, "I built this company from the ground up in the last ten years. I want team players."

"Well," Employer tells Mr. Eager, "we might be able to meet that. Let's keep talking."

Sounds promising, but when all is said and done, Employer picks Mr. Dedicated. "I want a 'company man,'" Employer reasons, "and I'm willing to go to the mid-forties to get him. After all, Mr. Dedicated must be worth at least as much as Mr. Eager."

Mr. Eager loses the offer.

Example 2: Ms. Polite Loses $2,500 a Year

Ms. Polite knows women make 59 cents to a man's dollar. She's got corporate aspirations, though, and a solid past to build them on. Now that an M.B.A. is added to the top of her resume, she's got the technical education to back up her ambitions. But the job market is tough, and competition is survival of the fittest.

"We're budgeted at $37,500 for this position, Ms. Polite," says Mr. S. Tablishment. "And we really shouldn't talk any further unless that figure fits your requirements."

"Hmmm," Polite thinks, "not quite what I expected, but no use quibbling now, I want to stay in the running! I can't reject it. Better give in here and negotiate later."

"That seems fair," she says. "Tell me more about the qualities you're looking for."

Thursday, Ms. Polite's phone rings: "Mr. Tablishment calling." He says his firm is offering her the job, but she should decide right away, because he has to contact the other candidates.

"Oh my," she thinks. "If I push now, I might lose the offer. Better say yes and negotiate a raise later based on my performance."

On Friday Mr. Tablishment tells his comptroller, "Harry, I know we had $40,000 set aside for the new position, but you can put $2,500 of that into my travel and entertainment budget. I've found someone with real potential, and she'll start at $37,500."

Ms. Polite loses $2,500 *each year*, and all the raises based on that.

Example 3: Mr. Hardwork Loses His Raise

Mr. Hardwork is hoping for a big raise this year. His accounts have perfect records, 10-percent better profits than last year, and several customers have written to the company to say what a conscientious job he's doing.

The raise is a week overdue, actually, because his boss has been discussing raises and overall compensation with the board since January, and the grapevine has rumored that the raises will surface on Ground Hog Day.

On February 9, Hardwork finds a note in his mailbox praising him for all the fine work this year, and acknowledging his wonderful contributions. It also informs him that he has been awarded a "very generous" 5-percent raise.

Hardwork feels cheated. He storms into his boss's office and complains bitterly about how unfair this is. He deserves at least 10 percent for his outstanding work.

"Gosh," says the boss, "we've really gone over all the records thoroughly. The board and personnel have looked at them and consulted industry standards. That's the best we can do. But tell you what, I'll talk one-on-one with the C.E.O., and mention you specifically, and we'll see what we can do."

Mr. Hardwork never got that extra 5 percent, and he didn't think to make it up by negotiating perks like vacation time, education, car, health club membership, bonuses, and IRA contributions.

Mr. Hardwork loses half his raise.

Don't let this happen to you.

The Principle of Quality

Winning at salary and raise negotiations involves, first of all, understanding the principle of quality.

"Quality is remembered long after price is forgotten," I was told by an accomplished salesman who was a client of mine. He reminded me that the many "bargains" I'd picked up in my life had worn out quickly, broken, or performed only after silent prayers or loud curses. I then remembered the other times when I paid dearly for the "top of the line." Almost every one of those tools, appliances, and clothes are still with me. Each time I use or wear them I relish the craftsmanship and care, admire the fit and effectiveness, and appreciate the durability and reliability.

Compensation negotiating is about those kinds of purchases. It is about the joy and satisfaction you will bring to employers when they see their investment in quality—you—compounded daily, easing their minds, making their business more money.

Smart employers know there's no free lunch. In the age of employee-owned companies like People Express, popular management books like Peters' *In Search of Excellence* (New York: Harper & Row, 1982), and cultural studies like Toffler's *The Third Wave* (New York: Bantam, 1984), employers know that human resources are the most valuable elements in a successful enterprise. On the one hand, they understand that they have to pay quality prices for quality personnel. On the other hand, since they are successful businesspeople, they try to get the best quality for the lowest price.

Their job is to make good business deals. *Your* job is to see that they recognize your quality and pay you your best price.

If you don't, it can cost you thousands of dollars and a big chunk of your self-esteem.

Let me show you how much better your working life can be when you do it the right way.

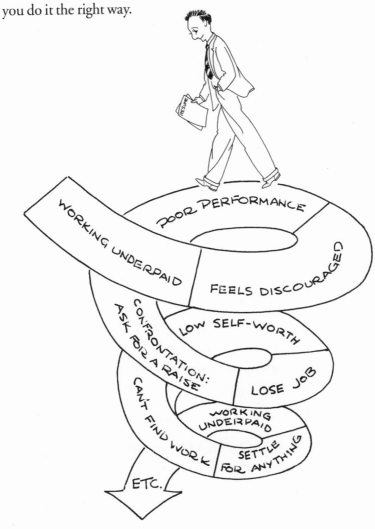

Entrenched in the vicious cycle.

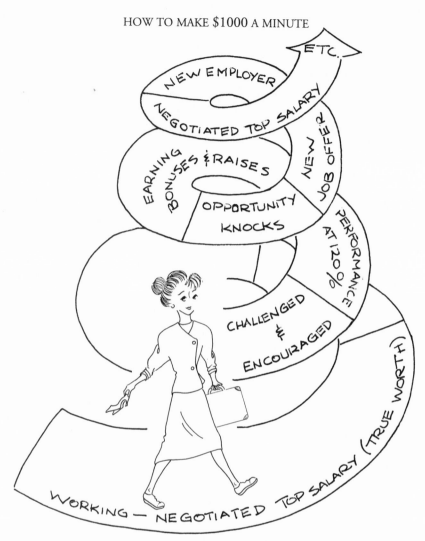

The virtuous cycle of Ms. Worth.

The Difference Between Vicious and Virtuous Cycles

First consider the vicious cycle: Mr. Drone is working, underpaid, and undervalued. His attitude is less than 100-percent enthusiastic and of course his work shows it. His co-workers and boss notice it, too, and the boss is secretly glad she didn't go that extra 10 percent because, after all, Drone is performing only adequately.

"Raise?" she says. "Clean up these performance reviews, and we'll consider it."

Maybe Drone says, "I quit!"

Perhaps the boss retorts, "You're fired."

Or maybe Drone just quietly shuts down. He does his job absent-mindedly, waiting for the moment when he and Walter Mitty walk out on the place during the busiest day of the year. "Then they'll miss me," he says. "They'll be sorry!"

Sooner or later, one way or another, Drone is out the door. To be polite, his employer gives him an innocuous letter of recommendation damning him with faint praise. Drone and his ego, a little worse for wear, hit the job market, wondering, "Am I really worth that extra 10 percent?"

Drone sheepishly lies when interviewers ask, "What was your last salary?" And since they're human, they pick up that either Drone didn't make that much, or that he isn't convinced that he was worth it.

A few desperate weeks pass. Drone's ego, once tall, is now barely crawling into interviews. Finally, someone offers him a job! Not quite what he expected, but it beats unemployment, and maybe *this employer* will notice his value and give him more money later.

The vicious cycle begins again, a little more entrenched.

Ms. Worth

Now consider the virtuous cycle, the story of Ms. Worth. She negotiated for top dollar in her first position. Her boss knew Worth was expensive, but convinced himself she was worth it, and placed serious responsibilities in her job. Encouraged by her boss's trust and challenged by the work, Worth extends herself, and puts out 120 percent, tucking success after success under her belt.

The boss is thrilled, but worried after a year of such performance: Worth is such a talented person, she might move on. So the boss gives her a raise and a hefty bonus to keep her happy, but to no avail. One of Worth's coworkers is impressed with her quality and praises her to a friend, who is connected to a Mr. Jones, who is looking for someone just like Worth. Jones is willing to be flexible on the compensation if the quality is there.

"Sure, let's talk," says Worth.

And the virtuous cycle starts again—happily, a little more en-trenched.

Both these scenarios hinge on salary negotiations. When you negoti-ate for your true value, both you and your company will win.

CHAPTER TWO

Aiming for What You're Worth

Good negotiations, like Ms. Worth's, are ones where both sides applaud the outcome. These employees feel appreciated and motivated, while their bosses feel they've hired someone of quality who's worth every penny. Obviously, it pays to follow Worth's example and go for top dollar.

But how do you know what top dollar is? How will you know what's too little? Is it possible to reach for too much? In other words, how can you tell what you are really worth?

To find out, we need to look first at the situation through the employers' eyes, and bring up the three principles they keep in mind when budgeting a salary or raise.

Labor is Intangible

Salesmen will tell you there are two kinds of products: tangibles and intangibles. The first principle employers consider is that a person's labor falls in the intangible category.

Determining the price of a tangible is easily done by applying this formula:

RAW MATERIALS + PRODUCTION COSTS + 10% PROFIT = SELLING PRICE

For intangibles, the first two variables in that equation are zero.

Your labor is even less like a tangible TV or car because even when a deal is struck, the "product" (your work) is "subject to change without notice," since it is entirely under your control. The more you can do, the more complicated problems you can solve for someone, the more your labor should be worth. Measuring that worth is difficult. There's a whole specialty of professionals devoted to just that. They're called compensation analysts. All they do day after day is figure out how much people should get paid.

But employers know that even when a compensation analyst has set a figure for a particular job, it's only an educated guess, a guideline. Some workers are worth several thousand more, because they do that much more, while others accomplish less and therefore deserve smaller checks.

Since labor is an intangible, employers know there's no fixed price, no number chiseled in granite. Rather there is a range.

Salary Relates to Level of Responsibility

The employer's second principle is: The main variable that determines compensation is the employee's degree of responsibility. The more people or products an employee's decisions affect, the more money they influence, as well. Salary is merely a reflection of that responsibility.

The typists in a law firm, for instance, have little effect on business. Others decide what they will type, and still others check their work. The paralegal's research, however, actually helps win a case. And the associate attorney's contribution is crucial to getting the case resolved. But it is the experience, courtroom savvy, and legal thinking of the partners, who consult with and direct the associates, that ultimately pay all their salaries. If they win the case, everyone will share the glory; if they lose, the partners will take the blame. They shoulder the most responsibility, and they make the most money.

Likewise Lee Iacocca's decisions can win or lose millions of dollars in an instant, and his salary reflects that colossal responsibility. Experienced securities analysts, too, earn six figures, but only because their decisions earn nine figures for the portfolios they direct.

The Universal Hiring Principle Is "Make Me a Buck"

The employer's third principle, the universal hiring principle, I learned from Tom Jackson. In my words it's very simple: "Make me a buck."

This principle seems to say that if you show employers you'll make them even $1 more than you cost, they should hire you. In actual practice, however, when you add up telephones, desk space, support staff, equipment, hiring costs, training costs, medical benefits, standard perks and vacations, and other expenses, *your decisions and labor usually must gross a company three to five times your salary to make hiring you worth their while.*

I've often had clients tell me, "Oh, I don't know if I could ever take one of those commission jobs. I need a secure income."

Hey! I've got news for them. We *all* work on commission. We all earn only a percentage of what we make for a company. Take a look at 1982, when the recession hit everyone's sales. Who lost their jobs? Commissioned salespeople? No, they just worked harder. It was the middle management, support staff, and CEOs who were no longer "cost-effective" and got their pink slips.

You either make more for your employer than you cost, or you go. Even charitable nonprofit agencies pay on commission. Either you contribute work that other people believe in and "pay" for with their charitable donations, or you turn nonprofit yourself.

Would you believe it's true in *government,* too? Government is the most immune to the profit principle because (a) it's supposed to provide public services, not make a profit; and (b) if it runs out of money, it can just levy and collect more taxes. How does "Make me a buck" apply there?

As far as elected officials are concerned, their salaries depend on the support of the voters. They will continue to get paid only if they are reelected, which is their reward for delivering or promising services that the people appreciate. To deliver those goodies from the public coffers, however, government eventually must either balance the budget (more or less) or raise taxes. And raising taxes can be the easiest way for politicians to fire themselves. If an official pushes for something the voters (notice and) don't like: Poof! He or she is gone.

So political "Make me a buck" is more accurately expressed as "Make me a vote to make me a buck." Unless an employee is doing work that is cost-effective, within the budget, and likely to get the boss reelected, bye-bye!

When it comes to putting an actual dollar figure on a government employee's contribution, the federal government and most other government units have very rigid step and grade systems for compensating their bureaucrats. Since public service employees do not produce money but only transfer it from one citizen to another, there's no way to determine their profitability. So government typically looks to the profit-making sector, compares duties, chooses a salary, and locks it in. Therefore even the nonprofit sector gets paid by referring to the "Make me a buck" profit-making sector.

The employer's principle of making more for the company than you cost it is aptly illustrated by Example 4.

Million Dollar Blunders

Example 4: Mr. Greedy Gets What He Deserves

Mr. Greedy had a technical and managerial decision-making background worth $35,000 a year. His education supported this assessment, too. But he clearly had the potential to handle work worth $100,000 and up in the long run, and he was hard at work on his job search.

He approached a high-tech manufacturing firm to explore a very competitive position. After a thorough discussion, the head honcho said, "You aren't qualified for the big buck positions yet, but I think you have potential." He further hinted that if Greedy were willing to come aboard at a lower level and get some exposure and experience, perhaps he would have a competitive edge for future openings. "Of course," the president misguessed, "this lower-level production position would not pay you what you're worth, because we could only do $40,000 to $44,000 on it, but you could consider it."

Of course Greedy was ecstatic. The position paid almost $10,000 over his fondest hopes, for work that seemed like a piece of cake. Instead of being cautious at being overpaid, he let it stand that the forties was the range for him.

Well, Greedy's further discussions with the firm's senior managers left them less convinced of his long-term potential than the president had been.

Why, they reasoned, should we hand over $40,000 for a $25,000 production job when we don't know if this guy will really work out in the long term? They might have been quite willing to pay him $25,000 to $30,000 and judge his performance over time. However, the president had boxed the company in by committing to the $40,000 range, and Greedy had boxed himself in by agreeing too soon to be overpaid. So instead, they sent Mr. Greedy a TNT letter (Thanks, No Thanks) stating, "We do not see a match with your career goals and our firm at this time."

Greedy tried, of course, to defuse the salary issue, to claim that, actually, he'd consider *anything* to get into that field, but it was hard to do without sounding desperate or begging. These people were top-level executives and had no time to review this five-person decision further. So it goes.

Greedy should have defused the salary question right away. Instead of operating on a "get all I can principle," a quick comment like this might have kept the potential job alive: "Well, it's really too early to discuss salary—I would just want a fair salary for whatever responsibilities I handle. Let's first discuss how I can help you."

The Basic Principle of Effective Salary Negotiations

We've seen that when employers plan salaries and raises, they operate from three principles:

1. Labor is an intangible.

2. Salary relates to level of responsibility.

3. The employee must make the company money.

We've also noted that being greedy often boomerangs. So the answer to the question, "How much am I really worth?" is, "Only what's fair and competitive for your level of contributions in the job." And since your contributions are intangible, what's fair and competitive is not a fixed price, but a range. You should aim for the top of that range.

When you examine your present compensation, or look at a new salary, hold this attitude: "When I'm paid the very best my skills can get in the market, I've made a good bargain."

This is the basic principle of effective salary negotiations. It helps ensure that both sides will be happy. Good negotiations, after all, are always win-win negotiations.

In Chapter 5 we'll see how to research your market value so you'll know exactly what range to request for a specific position. Now, however, you're about to shake hands with Mr. Employer and step into his office.

CHAPTER THREE

Salary-Making Rule 1: When to Discuss It

Mr. Employer walks into the waiting room and introduces himself. You smile and shake hands. He leads you to his office, invites you to sit down, and then describes the job he's interviewing you for. Next he glances at your resume and poses a few questions about your qualifications. You do your best to convince him of your quality. Now, Mr. Employer looks you straight in the eye and asks, "By the way, what sort of salary are you looking for?"

What do you do?

Follow salary-making rule 1, which says that one time, and one time only, is right for talking salary. In a moment, I'll tell you exactly what that time is. For now, I'll just give you a hint: This is not it.

To understand why that's so, we first need to learn a funny yet true piece of human nature that applies to all of us, including Mr. Employer.

Ever Bought Something You Couldn't Afford?

There's a question I always ask in my seminars: "Have you ever bought something you couldn't afford?"

Every person pauses, looks blank for a moment, and then breaks into a nod and a smile as they remember the things they bought that they "couldn't afford." They pause because the left side of the brain, the logical side, knows it's a contradiction in terms: You can't buy something you can't afford; if you do, it means that you really *can* afford it. Then the right side of the brain, the feelings and visionary side, remembers the painful struggle, the exciting resolution, and the pleasure of the purchases they couldn't afford.

Do you own a house? Could you afford it when you first bought it? Do you own a car? Could you afford it when you bought it? Think of anything of really high quality that you have bought: a special vacation, for example. Before you decided to spend the money, did you think of yourself as someone who could afford that kind of thing?

How do people get to the point of buying something they can't afford?

Well, usually they progress from curious to interested, intrigued, wanting it, wanting it a lot, wondering how they can get it, thinking about it almost all the time, scheming, scrimping, saving, and, finally, buying it because they just can't *stand* it anymore! Then they wonder, "How did I ever get along without it?"

My term for this process is *Budget Bending*. During this process, as the urge to buy grows stronger, people make their money supply grow, too, by making it more flexible. We can divide this progressive flexibility into three stages that I call (1) **budget**, (2) **fudgit**, and (3) **judgit**.

The first stage is familiar to everybody. No matter at what point a new desire creeps in, it's met with money's first line of defense: the **budget**.

A budget is the way we hold on to the illusion that we are controlling our finances. In handling money we all like to feel in charge. The easiest way to do that is to count how many dollars come in, divide them up into little piles, and name one pile "rent," another "food," another "savings," and so on. So at the end of the month we have parceled up the income and transformed it into outgo and we're at zero again. We feel in control.

Now that's not really controlling our finances. It's like adding water to the soup until it's thin enough to give everybody a cupful, or like "steering" a canoe down the rapids.

But it's very comfortable to live out of a budget structure. It allows us "to not afford" things we are scared of, cry poor, complain about the economy, and lead a simple, organized existence at the same time. That's **budget**, or living within our means—the most rigid stage.

While we might love to own a Mercedes, our budget won't allow it and we leave it until the day we win the lottery. But our next-door neighbor gets a Mercedes, and then his neighbor does. We find ourselves reading the Mercedes ads instead of the business section in *Time*.

An increeping spending urge is met by money's first line of defense: The Budget.

This desire erodes our budget and slips us into **fudgit**, the financial status quo's next defense.

In the **fudgit** stage we still think income is constant, but we are willing to shuffle the outgo to make room for new things.

"Maybe if I quit smoking, walk to work, buy my clothes on sale, and deduct the car's principal and interest as business expenses, I too could buy a Mercedes." The key word here is *maybe*. Purchases are very rarely made in the **fudgit** stage. Since money is still not flexible, budget jug-

**Shuffling the outgo of money to make room for new things:
The Fudgit Stage.**

gling usually doesn't provide all the extra cash needed, but it gets you closer. Working through the **fudgit** stage gets you ready to take the plunge if the object goes on sale, or if you just can't stand it anymore.

However, the sure way to get from *maybe* to *yes* is by going through the **judgit** stage.

Say one day we casually ask our neighbor with the Mercedes how he can afford it. "Well, I'm in real estate," he says. "So I shut down the office, hired

18

In The Judgit Stage anything is possible, even a real estate office on wheels!

an answering service, and put a phone in the car. Now I run my business out of the trunk, so I save all that rent and other overhead. But that really doesn't cover it. The most important part is that when my clients see me in my phone-equipped Mercedes they are really impressed. My sales have doubled because people take me seriously, and referral business has tripled since I'm almost always there to answer the phone!"

Notice how the actual *quantity* of money available becomes flexible. The **judgit** stage takes an objective but creative look at the Mercedes and sees it not as a liability, but as a money-saving asset. Of course we can't afford it now, but the only way ever to afford it is to buy it! So in the light of long-term thinking we can be most expansive and flexible about the money.

The same thing happens when we decide to spend $5,000 on a new, efficient heating system we "can't afford." It will pay for itself over the next three to five years. We'll buy an item of superior quality now and save fuel and replacement costs later.

Waiting for the Right Moment

The best moment to talk salary with Mr. Employer is when he's reached the **judgit** stage. Let me show you why.

Employers are always curious about your most recent salary for just one reason: to screen you. When faced with a lot of applicants, they use salary as a quick, shorthand way of assessing the fit and narrowing down the list.

They don't want to waste interviewing time, so they screen out people they "can't afford." They also cross off people who are below their range. They can afford those people, but since salary is related to degree of responsibility, employers think someone earning less than the budgeted range probably couldn't handle the job. Restricting interviews according to salary, therefore, is intended to get the most competent help for the least possible money. This is the employer's **budget** stage.

While screening for the cheapest capable candidate, however, the boss or personnel officer may scratch you off the list regardless of whether you could really do the work or are even the best person for the job. Even if you pass the screening, you'll be locked into the figure you quoted and will lose the opportunity to get the best market price for your skills.

Is it ever in your interest to be screened? If you're qualified for the job, NO. Don't talk salary yet.

Salary-making rule 1 is: Never discuss salary until you have been offered the job.

When Mr. Employer offers you the job, he's either *in* the **judgit** stage, or as close to it as he's going to get. He's convinced you're the best candidate. Therefore he's more willing to make the pay scale flexible—and even practice creative budget juggling—to get you.*

There's another reason to postpone salary discussions until the job has been offered. Let's take an example from your own shopping experience.

If you want to buy a tape player, you check out several stores. Suppose every salesman quotes a price except one, who says, "Look, here is what I have, I think it's the quality you want. So if I'm right, before you buy anywhere else, come back and talk to me about price. I'm sure we can

---

*The same applies to raises. There the rule would be: Never discuss a raise until you've had your review. If your performance review has impressed the boss, he'll be poised at the judgit stage, ready to be flexible about money. Since you've convinced him of your quality, it's as if he's "rehiring" you by granting you a raise.

make a deal." Would you at least check in there before buying if you thought he'd give you the best price? Of course. But if he had already quoted $119, and in your fourth store you saw the equivalent for $125, would you bother to go back for $6.00? Probably not. Keeping a price flexible and open motivates people to check back before deciding.

So if you table salary negotiations until you have a nod from potential employers, they're likely at least to check back with you before their final round.

But what if the job doesn't pay in your range anyway? Aren't you just wasting your time and theirs by interviewing? Yes. But what in the world are you doing interviewing for a job below your level of responsibility? You'd better do some homework or hire a career consultant to get you on track. You should be able to screen the job in terms of how much responsibility it requires. If it's at a level where you're comfortably challenged, the right money should follow.

How to Postpone Salary Talk: Part I

By now you may be thinking, "Okay, it sounds like a good idea to put off discussing salary until I've been offered the job. But how do I do that? When Mr. Employer asks me right away what salary I'm looking for, I can't just ignore the question."

True. Here's what you do. You can respond confidently to any premature salary gambit with the response, "I'm sure we can come to a good salary agreement if I'm the right person for the job, so let's agree on that first." Or "Salary? Well, so far the job seems like it's the right level of responsibility for me, and I'm sure you pay a fair salary, don't you?" (What can he say?) "So let's table salary until you know you want me. What other areas should we discuss now?"

Some of my other clients have answered the question, "What are your salary requirements?" with "Are you offering me the job?"

Other handy phrases can be found at the end of the next chapter. There are many polite ways to postpone salary talk. These delays in discussing money can give you time to move your potential employer from **budget** to **fudgit** to **judgit.**

What if They Get Mad at Me?

Chapter 10 covers handling this worry in more detail. For now, let's look at how we might avoid any struggle at all!

Admittedly it feels a little tense when an employer asks about your salary requirements and you won't disclose them.

A tug-o-war over disclosing your money requirements *hurts* your chances of being hired because it destroys the rapport needed for hiring. Your Rule of Thumb here is to put off the first request, maybe the second, but if asked a third time, you'll need to handle it more directly.

Here are ways to handle it and avoid a struggle:

A) Soften your "Let's wait" statements with introductory phrases like:

"Discussing salary is always awkward for me, . . ."

"I know you must be eager to know my requirements, but . . ."

"Could I say something about that? . . ."

"When we discuss money up front I get worried I'll be screened out or boxed in, so could we . . ."

B) Use questions to find out what's so important?

"I've noticed we're back on salary again, may I ask you a question? (OK) Are you wondering if you can afford me? or just need it for an application? or something else?"

"I've noticed we've come back to salary; I'd like you to know that I'd be glad to talk about money, and even share my tax return with you at some point if it's important, but could we take a moment to talk about why we need to discuss this now?"

C) Finally, it's a free country! So you can "disobey" my salary making rules altogether and reveal your salary upfront. That will also end a tug-o-war. You always have that option available to you and I even discuss how in Chapter 10. *I don't recommend it, however.*

For now, keep reading! At the end of the next chapter I describe how others have said it. Learn rules 2-5. If you allow the right mindset to develop, you'll find your own natural words and ways to postpone salary talk.

If you need any help, encouragement, practice, or coaching, there is a special telecoaching service for my readers described in Chapter 11. Take advantage of it.

Development of an Offer

With the right research and approach, the tactics discussed above can even allow you strategically to explore positions seemingly beneath you.

For instance, I had a client with top management capabilities who chose to interview for a line manager position paying way below his worth. While normally this would be a waste of time, by applying proper salary talk timing, he was able to develop it into a superior offer. Here's his own account:

"My interview was with the vice president of operations. He said the slot he wanted to fill was operations manager, salary $22,000. When he asked if that salary would be okay, I said I wanted to table salary discussions until we were sure I was right for the job. Then while he talked about the company, I made mental notes about its problem areas, to go along with what I'd learned by reading the company literature and talking to the secretary.

"He asked what my strengths were, and I told him the top four. He asked what my weaknesses were, and after about a fifteen-second pause I said I'd need additional time to think of a weakness with respect to this position.

"After more discussion about my background, which I related to company problem areas, he offered me the position of district manager at a salary of $30,000 to $35,000.

"Once again, I declined to discuss salary. Instead I steered the conversation back to four of their stores in South Carolina, which I knew from my research were ineffectively managed. I pointed out qualifications listed on my resume that coincided with that need.

"Then he asked me how much I actually wanted in salary. I answered that I felt my salary should be based on the responsibilities of the job and the standards of the industry.

"After that he began talking about an even better job concerning the four problem stores. He said that the job, on approval of the president, could pay $40,000 to $45,000!

"An interview that was only supposed to take thirty minutes actually took ninety, and my interviewer said he'd talk to the president about paying top dollar for top people."

Another client deliberately interviewed for an advertised position as a computer aided design (CAD) manager, pegged at $40,000 a year. He followed up the interview with a letter telling how he could: (a) solve the problems they had talked about, (b) solve some other problems they had hinted at, and (c) help over the next two years to integrate the CAD with the CAM (computer aided manufacturing) systems, saving the company untold grief and overhead.

If he had revealed his salary requirements in the beginning, he'd have been screened out while the company was in the **budget** stage and never been hired in the **judgit** stage at $65,000.

Seller/Buyer Role Reversal in Negotiations

Finally, common sales sense says you'll get your best money if you wait. An interesting role reversal takes place if you postpone salary discussions until offer time.

Interviews start with employers buying and you selling. If you (even passively) agree to an X dollar price or range for the offer, they line up their candidates and pick one and say, "Okay, I'll buy you for X dollars." If you postpone discussing salary, however, the role is reversed. They are in a position where *they* want *you.* They have judged your quality, not your price. They've decided to ask you to join them, so they're selling the job to you! They are motivated at this time to offer you their best price, because they want your contribution. If they aren't beyond the **budget** stage yet, this is the only time they'll be motivated to break through it.

So be prepared when Mr. Employer looks you in the eye and says, "What sort of salary are you looking for?" Ask yourself whether he's in the **judgit** stage. Remember that salary-making rule 1 is: Never discuss salary until you have been offered the job.

CHAPTER FOUR

Salary-Making Rule 2: Who Goes First

"What will it take to bring you aboard?" Mr. Employer asks.

"Are you offering me the job?"

"Yes!"

Now what? Should you answer the question?

Let's calculate the odds of coming out ahead if you go first. Keep in mind that your work and dedication are intangible and difficult to price. That means there's a range. Even if the employer is in the **budget** phase, there is still a range with which to work. Let's say, for example, that the company's range for this job is $25,000 to $30,000. If you go first you can only be, as Goldilocks might tell you, too high, too low, or just right. Let's see what happens.

Calculating Winning Odds of the First Move

You Go First—Too High

You think, "Okay, you dirty chiseling rats, I know you're out to steal me cheap, but I'm too smart for you." In your most diplomatic tones you say, "I know what I'm worth, and I want $35,000 to accept your offer."

The response? Probably, "Sorry, wrong number."

Your comeback: "Aw! I was just kidding, I really would accept $34,000 ... $33,000? ... $32,000 sounds reasonable ... $31,000? Gee, would you believe I love this place so much I'd go as low as $30,000?" Sound like begging? Awkward, isn't it? So you lose the offer, or beg for the job.

YOU GO FIRST—TOO HIGH. THE OUTCOME:

WINS	LOSSES
O	The Job and Your Dignity

Actually the rejection might be phrased like this: "Well, $35,000 is really not in our range, so give me some time to talk to our comptroller about it and get back to you, let's say, Thursday." (Don't hold your breath.)

You Go First—Too Low

You think, "Listen, Scrooge, you may get Bob Cratchit for peanuts, but you're paying me a fair wage." Firmly you say, "I know how valuable I am, and I won't touch your job for less than $20,000."

Mr. Employer is disappointed. He thought he was finally getting quality and finds out you are a low-priced spread. "Well," he replies, "that really is not in our range, so give me some time to talk to our comptroller about it and get back to you, say, Thursday." (Again, don't hold your breath.)

Or he might say some version of "SOLD!" like, "Hmmm, $20,000, well that will stretch our budget, but I think we can come up with it for someone of your quality. When would you like to start?"

YOU GO FIRST—TOO LOW. THE OUTCOME:

WINS	LOSSES
O	The Job
The Job	*$5,000 to $10,000*

You Go First—Just Right

What if you're just right? That is, you happen to hit the top of the range: "This will cost you $30,000, Mr. Employer."

"Hmmm, that will really stretch our budget," Mr. Employer says, "but I think we could come up with that for someone of your quality. When would you like to start?" Sound familiar? Of course. It's the "too low" response. So even if you were just right, you'll always wonder if you were really too low!

26

YOU GO FIRST—JUST RIGHT. THE OUTCOME:

WINS	LOSSES
The Job	$?????

So salary-making rule 2 is: *Let them go first.*

If you go first, you can choose from among these outcomes: lose the job, lose both the job and your dignity, lose $5,000 to $10,000, or not know whether you've lost or won. Not very encouraging odds. Besides, it's not even your place to go first. If you followed salary-making rule 1, they are the seller now. It is the seller's responsibility to name the price.

When you go to buy a new suit and find one that's right you ask, "What's it cost?" Does the seller reply, "Well, how much have you got?" or "What did you pay for your last suit?" It's not *your* job to figure out how much this job is worth to these people in this situation at this time. (You do need to know your market value, of course. We'll get to that in Chapter 5.) Employers know their business plans. They should have an idea of how you can make or save them a buck. It's their place to tell you.

How to Postpone Salary Talk: Part II

In *Harvey*, people were moved by the lost-child look of Elwood P. Dowd to ask, "Can I help you?" He always replied, "Why sure, what did you have in mind?" Keep that phrase handy! As in, "Well, I'm sure you have something budgeted for this position. What range did you have in mind?" Or, "I have some idea of the market, but let's start with your range for the moment."

Some interviewers may be very persistent about knowing your range or previous salary. Usually this happens prior to an offer, and this is covered by salary-making rule 1. Remember, discussing salary before an offer is just another way for you to go first. Here are a few more of the ways you can postpone salary discussions to make sure they go first.

Some clients, when asked about present salary say, "I'm paid very fairly for my responsibilities in my present job, and I expect a fair salary with respect to my responsibilities here." They continue by saying,

> (If there's been no offer yet) "Let's keep talking to make sure I'm the one you want."

(If an offer has been made) "What did you have in mind?"

When asked the second or third time for his salary, one client of mine finally just ignored it. A second said, "Hell, it don't make no diff'rence what I was a-makin' before, it's what *you're* gonna pay me that counts, ain't it?"

A third client took up the issue head on. "Maybe you've noticed by now that it's a clear principle of mine never to discuss salary up front. If we're going to work together, we'll have to respect each other's principles, won't we? So let's see how I can help you make (or save) money."

Another client, when questioned by a personnel representative about his present salary said, "I don't have to answer that, do I?" "No," the personnel rep replied, "I just have to ask it."

The best postponing phrase speaks *confidence* in being hired. For example, "I'm sure we can come to a good salary agreement when the time comes." Often a statement like this will set your interviewer at ease: "Don't worry about salary—I know I need to make you more than I cost. Let's make sure the fit is right."

If you have some experience of your own as an interviewer, you could say, "Look, if salary is all you're worried about, there's no problem! When I hired people myself, salary is just the finishing touch to the person who can really play for the team. Let's talk about it when we're sure I'm the player you're after."

Here are some additional examples that show you can invent your own phrases rather than reciting someone else's.

Nancy, who had been underpaid in a previous position, and had run her own business for two years, handled salary questions like this: "I don't want to appear difficult. I can understand that you want to be sure you can afford me, and I won't require a salary out of line with the job. But it is a principle of mine not to discuss salary yet, because it can throw us off the track. What's really important is whether I'm right for the job and what I can produce for you."

When Denny was asked his salary expectations, he replied, "Well, compensation is about number 3 on my priorities list right now. Number 1 is making sure we can work together, and I'd just as soon concentrate on that for now, if you don't mind." Denny was able to boost the employer's limit of "$40,000, tops" to $60,000 and bonuses!

After her boss declared, "Raises will be 5 percent across the board this year," Helen said, "I'm not interested in discussing raises yet. First let's make sure our goals match up. Then if we need to figure out raises, we'll have something to go on." Instead of a 5-percent raise, Helen got a new **judgit** salary, 18 percent higher than her old one, to go with a new job title and responsibilities.

One of my favorite postoffer responses is, "Me mention a figure first? Well, I'm firm on one point, so let's get that one perfectly clear. I have absolutely no upper limits. Now what did you have in mind?" If you need personalized advice for negotiating a salary, call the telecoaching service described in Chapter 11.

All right. Let's return to Mr. Employer's office. He's offered you the job and urged you to say what salary you'll accept. You know, though, that there's nothing to gain by going first. Therefore, you've confidently asked him to name his opening bid.

Sure enough, he drums his fingers on the desk, clears his throat, and states a price. Now it's your move again. What do you do?

You follow an ingenious and proven strategy called salary-making rule 3.

CHAPTER FIVE

Salary-Making Rule 3: Your First Response

In my job as a career consultant, where everything I do is individualized and there are exceptions to every rule, it's delightful to know that salary-making rule 3 always holds. Salary-making rule 3 is: When you hear the figure or range, repeat the figure or top of the range, and then be quiet.

Dangers and Power of Silence: Out for the Count

You must repeat the figure or top of the range with a contemplative tone in your voice, as though this were the start of a Camp David summit meeting. Your enthusiasm for the job and company and industry has been unbounded up to this point. Now let a quiet look of concern grace your countenance, and gaze at your slightly shuffling feet as you ponder this offer. Count to thirty, and think.

First you should calculate exactly what the offer is. For example, you can easily convert an hourly figure to a yearly figure by doubling it in thousands: $5 an hour is $10,000 a year, roughly. $12 an hour is $24,000, $15 an hour is $30,000. These are based on forty hours per week with no overtime. To go from weekly to yearly, multiply by fifty: $300 a week is $15,000 a year, and so on.

Calculate what the salary is and then compare it to your expectations of what this job should pay—considering your quality. During this time there is silence in the room. If you had not repeated the figure or the top of the range, the silence would be awkward or dangerous. Your interviewer would wonder if you had gone to sleep or if you'd heard

Let a quiet look of concern grace your countenance as you ponder the offer. Count to thirty, and think.

what they'd said. They might think you were accepting it or that you're too shy to talk about money.

But when you repeat it, they know that you heard it, and they think you are disappointed. Let them be nervous, worried, or anxious so that they carefully consider your quality and the return you would make on their investment.

The most likely outcome of this silence is a raise. How about that! You haven't even been on the job for thirty seconds and already you have a raise. It might sound like, "(silence) . . . But we could go as high as $ _____ for someone like you," or, "(silence) . . . But we could be flexible on that." If you like you can greet the raise with the same silent treatment: "$30,000. Hmmm! (silence)."

Sometimes you'll get an explanation of why their budget only allows this much. "Times are rough, competition's tough, we've just sunk money into an updated Flam-a-doodle Wig Whumper, and the cash flow is squeezed by the president's business trip to Hawaii last month."

Listen. Be quiet. Think. Play Buddha.

Compare, contrast, evaluate, and then respond.

What do you respond with? The truth.

Responding with the Truth

The truth is either "sounds great," "sounds acceptable," or "sounds disappointing." You'll know which one is correct, because before the interview you'll have researched the going rate for skills such as yours in jobs such as this: in other words, your market value. You'll have the strength and power to negotiate for your full value because you'll have the knowledge to back it up (the same goes for raise negotiating).

Note that your past or present salary is only one indication of your market value. Earlier you learned not to let your most recent salary limit your new one. If this offer is less than your most recent salary, you must abide by the same rules. It's not fair to say, "But that's less than I'm earning now," or "That's less than I earned before." Your salary in some other job has no bearing on your work with these people.

So don't compare the offer with your most recent salary. Instead, use the thirty seconds to compare their offer with your research.

Compendium of Salary Research Sources and Methods

There are several ways to research salary information.*

Printed Material Research

Hit the books! Your library has lots of lists and books about who makes what. For starters, every library will have the *Occupational Out-*

---

* The first and second methods, "Printed Material Research" and "Professional Associations and Trade Journals," are for those who have plenty of time; if you face a salary discussion soon, however, the "Direct Dial Research" described on page 38 is a faster way to get your information.

look Handbook. This is commonly called the O.O.H., and your taxes pay people to research and publish this crystal ball. You're welcome to pay for it again by purchasing it from the U.S. Government Printing Office, Washington, DC 20402.

The volume describes tomorrow's jobs, and comments on each with respect to the nature of the work, places of employment, necessary training, other qualifications, advancement, present and future employment outlook, and—what you've been waiting for—earnings.

The O.O.H. is primarily a tool for entry-level people. Since it prognosticates on 300 different occupations in 600 pages, the information is very basic. Take a look at this excerpt from a typical entry:

Business Machine Repairers

Business machine repairers maintain and repair the machines that are used to speed paperwork in business and government.

Information from employers indicated that trainees started at over $____ a week in [year]. Even during training, salaries are often increased as workers sharpen their skills. People who have previous electronics training generally receive somewhat higher beginning wages than high school graduates.

Experienced repairers earn from $___ to over $____ a week . . .

If you are entry level, the O.O.H. can help you choose occupations that will pay decently.

Most libraries will have salary overviews like:

Paychecks: Who Makes What? David Harop, (New York: Harper & Row, 1980).

What Women Earn. Thelma Kandel, (New York: Simon & Schuster, 1981).

American Almanac of Jobs & Salaries. John W. Wright, (New York: Avon, 1984).

They will probably also have the *National Survey of Professional, Administrative, Technical, and Clerical Pay*, issued each year by the U.S. Bureau of Labor Statistics. You can get your own copy of this by sending $4 to U.S. Department of Labor, Bureau of Labor Statistics, Room 3400, 1515 Broadway, New York, NY 10036. Make checks payable to "Superintendent of Documents."

The survey covers far fewer jobs than the O.O.H. (around twenty-five), but the salary information about each is much more detailed. For example, let's look at the way it determines secretaries' wages:

Clerical positions are divided into five levels, each with a precise definition and a distinct salary range. The level of the clerical job depends on two factors: the status of the boss and the responsibilities of the job. So the survey defines three levels of bosses (roughly equivalent to line management, middle management, and executive) and four levels of responsibilities (from gofer to executive's right hand) and makes a grid like this:

Level of Secretary's Supervisor	Level of Secretary's Responsibility			
	LR-1	LR-2	LR-3	LR-4
	Level of Position as It Relates to Salary			
LS 1	I	II	III	IV
LS 2	I	III	IV	V
LS 3	I	IV	V	V

To give you a clearer idea of the survey's structure, the Appendix of this book quotes the full section on secretaries.

Charts 1-3, also in the Appendix, will give you an idea of the survey's graphs. You'll find the salary ranges for clerical levels I-V on Chart 3. Charts 1 and 2 contain ranges for professional and technical occupations and administrative occupations, respectively.

Keep in mind that the salary figures are national averages. If you live in an area where salaries are higher than the national average, the figures may be too low. If you live in an area where salaries are lower than the national average, the figures may be too high. The difference can be as much as 10 percent. Since the bureau also publishes regional surveys, however, you can reduce that margin of error by looking up the survey that covers your own area.

Professional Associations and Trade Journals

Professional associations are another salary information source. You can find the association you want by looking in your library's copy of:

The Encyclopedia of Associations. Denise Akey, ed., Gale Research Co. (Detroit, MI: Book Tower, 48226).

This book lists more than 18,000 professional organizations. Volume 1 lists the national organizations of the United States and gives a brief abstract of each one; Volume 2 lists organizations by geographical area, and gives the names and addresses of the executives in each organization.

If you are a glib talker, you can call up an association's headquarters and coax the receptionist, librarian, or director into giving you opinions or research data on salaries of the position you're considering.

Larger libraries, including university libraries, have extensive collections of trade journals, some of which are published by associations. These journals often have an issue with a salary survey—usually once a year.

Other magazines have salary surveys, too, so look in the Readers' Guide to Periodical Literature under "salaries" or "earnings."

Word-of-Mouth Resources

Besides association members, sources of money talk outside the library include recruiters, employment agents, personnel professionals, and your own network.

Read the section in Chapter 8 about discussing salary at networking interviews. Your network can give you not only information about salary ranges, but also advice to determine where you fit into those ranges.

Recruiters, job and career counselors, outplacement counselors, and employment agency counselors are all good sources of wage and earnings data. Recruiters generally specialize in a certain area of the job market, so you'd want to talk to one who knows your niche. The other counselors deal with a wide variety of clients, so their input won't be as detailed, but they are likely to know something about many different types of positions.

Ask around until you find someone who knows one of those professionals (or someone who knows someone who knows) and call them up. It's just a minute of their time, and if you indicate that you'll send the results of your research it's easily a fair trade.

Computers

Wouldn't it be great to be able to punch in some information and have a computer spill out a pay comparison analysis? For several years

Figure 5-1. Information required for a pay comparison.

When doing word-of-mouth and library research, and especially for Direct Dial Research, these are the factors to have in front of you:

My [potential] position or title is:

_____

_____

Level: ☐ Entry Level ☐ Middle ☐ Senior ☐ Not applicable.
How many years in job (if applicable)?:

_____

My three chief functions are [will be]:
1._____

_____

2._____

_____

3._____

_____

The person I [will] report to has the following title:

_____

[Potential] employer's main product, service, or field:

_____

Size (about how many employees, factories, branch offices, or if a hospital, beds, etc):

_____

(If known) Sales or revenue last year: $_____

City or region I [will] work in: _____

Additional comments (if any)

_____

_____

_____

_____

_____

you could. In my first edition, I included the phone number of an information bank in New York that for $25 provided a printout like the one in Figure 5-2. Such a deal!

Unfortunately, it went out of business. (I think it costs several times $25 to provide reliable salary information.) I have searched in vain to find another such service; as of this printing (1991) I have not found one. I include here an unabashed plea for help from my readers:

I know there is plenty of demand (calls still come in for the service), and if any of you know how it could be provided at a reasonable cost, call me at (312-346-5835) and we can discuss it. It would make a great joint-venture. Where there's a will, I'm sure there's a way.

In any event, Figures 5-1 and 5-2 show you the application sheet and printout sheet from the pay comparison analysis service while it was still in operation. Those two pages will serve as an outline of the kind of information that goes into making up a salary information request and therefore the kinds of things you should let someone know when doing your own salary survey (see "Word-of-Mouth Resources," and "Direct Dial Research"). The actual sample of a pay comparison analysis illustrates how defining the duties and level of the job can help set a salary range.

As an example, the pay comparison analysis and job description for career consultants in my type of firm is printed in Figure 5-2.

Direct Dial Research

For those of you who like to skip the intermediary, try a do-it-yourself method.

Say you're interviewing for a position as a customer service representative for an urban hospital. Pick out six places that would have similar positions, perhaps a medical clinic, a for-profit hospital a non-profit religious hospital, a unionized company, and a medium-sized local chain of stores.

Call each of them and ask to talk to their customer service representative. Explain to that person that you're negotiating a position similar to theirs and name the responsibilities. Say that you'll be calling five people from their city to find out comparable salary ranges, and if they participate in your survey you'll be glad to send them the results. You might

1986 PAY COMPARISON ANALYSIS
Data Prepared March 10, 1986 for . . .

Mr. Jack Chapman

Duties performed: Career Counselor
Reports to/Title: Director of Services
Type of business: Career Counseling
City (or region): Chicago
Code/Profile Data: 16622701.REP

How We Match Pay, Title, and Job

You may have a title that doesn't fit the work you do. If so, we will suggest a more appropriate title and we will supply the pay range for the actual work being done. Since no two employers are exactly alike, the job description furnished below is a reasonable match if the employee is doing 66% or more of the duties outlined. The salary range shown is from our surveys of businesses, individuals, nonprofits, professional groups, government agencies, plus other national and regional sources.

JOB DESCRIPTION—FUNCTIONAL SUMMARY: Training & Development Rep

Confers with account executive, individual client, client-company personnel head, or program organizer. Tailors T&D or counseling to fit a targeted goal, schedule and budget. Identifies program focus: Management development, retooling, preventive or remedial training, crossplacement, outplacement, job hunt or career change. Prepares content of training. May coach individual client or group in how to handle job interviews. May help design or edit resumes. May select mailing list for job applications. On behalf of account workshops. May design forms to evaluate training for client in terms of cost-effectiveness, measurable productivity, enhanced income etc. Keeps abreast of new training methods.

In general, analyzes skills, abilities and other data pertinent to classifying, training and advancing client. Conducts training in a manner that positions trainees with skills that compare favorably to industry standards. May help write or upgrade client-company procedures manuals. May be involved in shaping client-company job descriptions, performance-evaluation criteria or incentive plans based on an analysis of training needs. May assist account team in "packaging" new counseling services.

TYPICAL RESPONSIBILITIES
1. Formulates counseling or T&D in conformity with selected instructional methods and program budget.
2. May be authorized to choose training format: Individual coaching, group lectures, demonstrations, etc.
3. Selects (and after use and evaluation) may recommend changes in teaching aids, handbooks, demonstration models, audio-visual media, reference works, and furnishings or equipment in the T&D/counseling.
4. May specialize in career counseling, management development, executive public-relations speaking skills, refresher training, employee health and safety practices, or upgrading displaced workers.
5. May help coordinate own or client customer-relations staff's handling of phone sales and transactions.
6. May brief, orient, or work with trainers, consultants, or lecturers from outside or other departments.
7. May conduct follow-up tests of trainees to measure retention, progress or overall effectiveness.

Average Salary Range:	AREA	LOW	MODERATELY LOW	MEDIAN	MODERATELY HIGH	HIGH
Senior Training Specialist:	Northeast	$ $		$	$	$

The Average Raise in this field is (basically an adjustment for cost-of-living inflation trends) 5%.

Merit-Pay is an addition raise based on above-average efficiencies, cost-reductions, productivity, etc. To add up how much to ask for (or to give) as merit pay, use the Workbook you get with your Subscription to PAY and RAISES Digest.

Bonus pay may be enhanced by negotiation procedures in PAY and RAISES. Typical bonus: 12-25% of salary.

Tax Bracket factor is the extra amount to be added to a pay increase to make up for "bracket creep": See your Workbook Edition of PAY and RAISES for how best to calculate this.

Court-case issues (if any) affecting pay in your field: See bulletins in your PAY and RAISES Digest.

**Figure 5-2. Sample salary comparison analysis
—see "Computers" section in Chapter 4 for details.**

wish to explain that their specific company name won't be mentioned, only the category, like "non-profit religious hospitals." Ask: "What range would this position pay in your organization?"

They'll participate because they're just as curious as you about their position and its worth in the open market. So keep your word and get correct addresses so you can send the results. You can also request the same information from company personnel representatives, if you prefer to talk with them. On the one hand, they may be more reluctant to divulge their company's private pay information; on the other hand, they may be more motivated to know the results of your research because they can use it in their jobs.

The advantages of this method are that you get up-to-the-minute, precise salary information tailored exactly to your location. The disadvantage is that the sample is so small that you might get inaccurate information. Coupling it with library research and networking would probably be the most complete method of all.

Your Own Opinion of Where You Fit

Say you've done your homework. You've used one or more of these methods: printed material research, professional associations, word-of-mouth resources, computer banks, and direct dial research. You've gleaned plenty of facts about the range other people are getting. Now you form an opinion of where you fit in that range. In effect you form a "range within a range" by deciding the highest figure you're worth and the lowest figure you'll accept.

Say the research range is $25,000 to $35,000. Decide what figures in that span represent you. Are you below average? Average? Above average? Or are your skills so good that your pay should exceed the range altogether?

Informal conversations with people in your field can help you decide (again, more on that in the Chapter 8 section, "Discussing Salary at Networking Interviews"). The decision, however, is yours. The clearer you are about your past accomplishments and future goals, the more clearly you can state your value to the company and get a salary or raise to match.

Your value can also depend on the organization's needs, and often those aren't clear until the **judgit** stage. When at the **budget** stage an employer asks your salary expectations, it's only logical to say, "I couldn't possibly tell you what I'm worth to you until I know the whole job and how much I can produce for your organization." You may have tirelessly researched your market value, but until the **judgit** stage arrives, your understanding of your value to the firm may be cloudy. Here's an example.

I had a client who applied for a job as a word processor, with a market value of $6 to $10 an hour. When asked at the start of the interview if $10 an hour was acceptable, she said, "If $10 an hour is a fair and motivating wage, of course it's acceptable, but I'd rather wait and discuss salary when we're both clear about what I can produce for you."

They continued talking. By the time the employer reached **judgit**, it was evident that besides word processing, the company needed help with organizing mailing lists, newsletter distribution, dealing with printers, and a marathon monthly production weekend that required extreme efficiency, patience, and coordinating and communication talents.

As a word processor, my client might have been worth just $10 an hour. But by adding those other responsibilities, she was worth much more. By waiting for the **judgit** stage, not only did her employer see it, but so did she!

So before you show up at Mr. Employer's office, you should have an opinion of your "range within the range." You should also be prepared to upgrade it according to the particulars of the job.

You now have adequate information for responding to a salary offer.

CHAPTER SIX

Salary-Making Rule 4: Your Research Response

Going for Top of the Mark

Grounded in your knowledge of the market value for the position and your ultimate knowledge of your quality, you've calculated two figures before going into the interview: the highest you're worth and the lowest you'll accept. So after silence, and perhaps your first raise, *you tell them* whether they are too high, too low, or just right.

Salary-making rule 4 is: *Counter their offer with your researched response.*

Your strategy here is to get your top figure in a way the employer thinks is fair.

Responding to the Offer
Too High

This is generally a pleasant problem, but it deserves more attention than you might think. Remember, you're not out to get every penny you can; you only want a fair salary to match your peak performance. If your employer is making an overpaid mistake they'll begin to feel ripped off, just as you would in the underpaid vicious cycle scenario in Chapter 1. They'll regret the deal and resent you in the long run. While you may be delighted with the first paycheck, eventually you'll find yourself trapped because you can't get another job without a pay cut, and you can't get promoted because your boss begrudges your cost already.

The other possibility is that you're unwittingly in over your head. If you expected twenty grand and you're offered forty grand, maybe you've impressed these folks beyond your capabilities. Although $800 a week looks nice, it could turn out to be more like $800 for one frustrating week and then back on the street.

A response to too high might be, "Well, that's a very fair, actually a wonderful, offer. I take it as an indication of your belief in me as one who can do the job. Let's get the benefits clear and I think we can make the deal."

Finish up the negotiations but provide yourself with time, as suggested in Chapter 7, before you finally accept the position. You'll need that time to make a special effort to research the position, both to make sure you can handle it and to find out why they're being so generous.

A client called me one day deliriously high with a 150-percent salary increase and a benefits package that equaled a 200-percent raise. I was worried. The job seemed okay, but I told him to go back and check it out. The employer was frank: "We believe high-tech corporations succeed because of teamwork and dedication. Our projects often take years to accomplish, and they keep us at the cutting edge of technical application. When we find someone we like, we want them for the long haul. We know our compensation is above market price, but we don't want our people looking. We need 100 percent of your energy and commitment, and we know we have to pay for it." FINE! Since we know the employer is happy, we're happy. It's a win/win situation, and we've negotiated right.

Too Low

When the offer's too low, don't give up! There are many ways to increase it. Your first response should be to acknowledge it. "$25,000 ... I appreciate your offer, Mr. Employer." Then refocus on your *interest* in the job. "And I'd love to work here ... " Then put out a statement you can both agree on. "And I'm sure you want to pay me a compensation that is fair and will keep me committed and productive, isn't that right?" (What can they say?)

"Well," you continue, "from my research I estimate that positions like this for someone with my qualifications are paying in the range of X to Y thousand dollars. What can you do in that range?"

The range you give will bracket the high end of your research. If your research uncovered a range of $25,000 to $28,000, bracket the high range by saying, "In the range of $27,000 to $30,000."

Typically your interviewer will respond by telling you what they can do in that range. Something, nothing, whatever. You're ready to continue an honest discussion in order to reach a common ground. Do your best here. Hold on to your researched worth, and keep talking to find a way to work it out so you both win. Keep a mutuality about the negotiations. Look for a "compensation that is both fair and will keep me committed and productive."

Notice how this negotiation compares with the "You go first" too high/too low scenarios. In either of those cases you could lose the job; here you have a firm job offer at X thousand dollars. If all further negotiating comes to nothing, you can't lose the job offer. You can always in the end say, "Well, uh, let's go with X dollars," or "No thanks." But it's *your* decision.

Sincere negotiations, in my experience, end up with a satisfying common ground 90 percent of the time.

Many people, though, think they'll lose an employer's respect if they talk very long about money. That's true *before* an offer, as we learned from salary-making rule 1, but after an offer it can actually increase respect. For example, one of my clients received an offer on the phone, and insisted on discussing it in person. After two hours of negotiating, he had an acceptable offer. He made an extra $5,000 a year in those two hours. The employer concluded the session with the comment, "If I had any doubts about you before, they are gone now. I *know* why I've hired you." My client had listened carefully to their opinions and offers, and had kept going back to a *researched* response.

Here's where your own estimate of your quality comes into play. If you researched a salary spread of $5,000, you'll want to ask for the top of the spread if you believe your expertise merits it. Otherwise you'll settle for a middle range. Even if you're "entry level," however, go for a grand or two above the bottom. Sell your ambition and potential. Whatever you do, DON'T SAY NO IN THE ROOM!

If you can't reach a mutually satisfying salary, you still have the lower offer. Let the employer sweat a little. Remember, they want you. Tell them that you're still very excited about the opportunity and that you both will want to think about it and talk again tomorrow or Friday. You've got nothing to lose! As you will see when you look over the list of benefits and perks in Chapter 7, there may be ways to make the compensation package correct even if the base isn't what you expected. Negotiating profit sharing, bonuses, stock options, vacation time, accelerated commission scales, an entertainment budget, or a company car, are some of the ways to build your compensation. You or they may need time to come up with the creative financing.

Just Right

This is unlikely. The first figure you hear from your employer is generally their lowest figure. Even if they're in a fit of ecstasy and fudging and judging to entice you into the company, they're still prudent businesspeople and haven't backed themselves into a corner. But if it does happen, and you're confident that you've researched correctly, take the same thirty seconds to think about it, and then say, "Your figure matches my research exactly. I think that's a perfect starting point. Since I expect to learn fast, work hard, and become very productive for you, I'd like to discuss scheduling a tentative raise to X thousand dollars in six months." This way you're not pushing for anything more than a fair salary, but you're still bringing in a potential raise.

Remember all the losses we counted in Chapter 4 for "You Go First?" Let's look at the scorecard this time. It's reproduced on the following page. What a difference when you let them go first, you count to thirty, and you counter their offer with your researched response.

THEY GO FIRST—THE OUTCOME

TOO HIGH:	WIN	LOSE
	The Offer	_____
	Several Thousand $ Extra	_____
TOO LOW:	WIN	LOSE
	The Offer	_____
	A Raise	_____
	Perks and Benefits	_____
JUST RIGHT:	WIN	LOSE
	A Review	_____

CHAPTER SEVEN

Salary-Making Rule 5: Clinch the Deal, and Deal Some More

Negotiating Bennies and Perks

Sometime during your postoffer silence your interviewer might say, "Now that might seem low, but keep in mind our liberal benefits program. Free beer at the company picnic, your own space in the parking lot, a half day off at Christmas and a full-page spread in the company newsletter." Don't let these incredible goodies distract you from your first priority: your take-home pay. First come to an agreement on things like salary, commissions, and bonuses. Then move on to the bennies and perks.

Bennies is slang for "benefits." *Perks* is short for "hiring perquisites." They are important for two reasons. First, they can complement a solid salary, making the total package even better. Second, if the salary you've been offered isn't quite what you expected, adding on some of these nontaxable extras can bring the entire offer very close to the figure you had in mind. This is the meaning of salary-making rule 5: Clinch the deal, and deal some more.

Study the following eight sections, which cover examples of typical bennies and perks you may wish to negotiate. You might choose not to discuss all of them at your first negotiating session. Bring up a few of the major ones and save the others for a second session. Don't worry if you can't resolve all of them right away either. Some may be new to your employers, and they may need a few days to see what's possible.

After the bennies and perks sections, we'll see why it's vital to take time to think it over, how to juggle two or more offers, and when to get it in writing.

Salary Reviews

The first thing to explore after negotiating your base salary is the salary review. One of the reasons for negotiating the best base salary first is that raises are generally computed as percentages on that base. The higher the base, the greater the 2-, 3-, or 10-percent raise will be.

In negotiating a review there are three areas to consider: (1) timing, (2) basis, and (3) percentage. While you can't come up with the actual percentage now (if you could there would be no need for a review later on), you can influence it by taking a look at the cost-of-living adjustment (COLA).

The COLA is an automatic raise in salary to compensate for inflation. If inflation is 10 percent one year, and your raise is 10 percent that year, then you haven't received a raise at all. You're simply being paid in purchasing power exactly what you earned the previous year. So you can bring up the subject of a review by talking about COLA.

You might say, "I expect that my salary will keep pace with inflation, so there will be a cost-of-living adjustment each year, won't there?" Once you get your potential employer to agree to COLA, then you have already raised the actual percentage of your next raise, because it will need to be computed and then added to the COLA. There are several cost-of-living adjustment indicators that the government publishes and the personnel department should be able to choose an appropriate one.

If you haven't got the base salary to the level that's acceptable to you, you might postpone discussion of the COLA and discuss the review process itself as a way to increase your salary. You might suggest that the employer hire you at the salary level you would like and then review your performance after six months to come up with a salary that feels fair. If that doesn't work, suggest that you split the difference. Try it for six months and go from there. Or you can start at the salary level you have been offered and negotiate for a review of your performance in six months. You might request a retroactive raise for that period, based on your performance.

Eli Djeddah, author of *Moving Up* (Berkeley, CA: Ten Speed Press, 1978), suggests that you bring up the question of a review this way: "While my starting salary is important, I am also very interested in the future, since I expect to work here quite a while. In six months, when we review my performance, will it be on my demonstrated worth, or just a mechanical procedure?" Your employer will certainly choose the former, Eli asserts.

The timing of the review depends on you. Whatever time you estimate you will need to show tangible results, double it to be safe, and ask for the review at the end of that time. You can suggest that during the first week on the job you or your employer can come up with a specific set of objectives that will be the basis for a review. This will demonstrate your conviction that salary should be the direct reflection of your contribution, not pie in the sky.

When you ask for a review in six months or any period shorter than a year, you may get objections concerning "company policy." Request a special exception because of your intention to really shine. You can say, "If we look at my performance in six months and I have not reached my objectives, it won't cost you a penny. If I do reach them, you will have made more than I cost anyway. Either way you win and I am motivated."

Sales Compensation

The next items to consider are commission rates or bonuses that you can earn. If you are in sales, you typically earn commissions. You can try to negotiate higher commission rates if you wish. If those are standardized and non-negotiable, try asking for a higher commission rate over a certain quota. For example, if normal sales commissions are, say, 5 percent, you can ask that sales over $50,000 be paid a 6-percent commission.

Sales compensation packages have several variations:

Straight commission

Variable commission

Draw against commission

Advance against commission

Base plus commission

Salary plus commission

Salary and bonus

Salary

Residuals

I will define them here and discuss the rationale behind each package.

Straight Commission: Your compensation is strictly a percentage of your sales. To many people this arrangement *seems* like the most risky, but it's actually the one most under your control. If you sell well you're safe; no one will fire you. Sometimes I wonder where people think a company's money comes from. Draws and advances are not gifts; they come out of *your sales.* They simply represent payment ahead of time of a portion of your future earnings. If you don't sell, you're no more secure on salary than on commission.

The best salespeople love straight commission because they know they get every dollar that's coming to them, and their income is entirely in their control. However, sometimes you can't make sales right away. When your sales cycle is lengthy straight commission is generally not workable.

Variable Commission: Same as straight commission, but the rate goes up or down depending on sales circumstances. You might be paid a higher commission on new accounts, on larger sales, or on total volume over a certain amount. Negotiating an increase in commission rate for top performance can be very lucrative and motivating.

Draw Against Commission: This is also straight commission, except the employer lets you draw a certain amount of money each pay period to help you get started. So if you have a $1000 draw and you only make $800 in commissions, you would get a check for $1000 and you would owe the company $200. Later when your commissions are $1,200, you pay the company back. Most draws are forgivable, that means that if the job isn't working out you could quit and not have to pay back any money you owed the company. Do check this out.

Draws may last for different lengths of time, and the draw itself may be reduced or increased over time.

Advance Against Commissions: Like a draw, but it is usually an occasional rather than an on-going event.

Base Plus Commission: Same as salary plus commission. Here the company pays you a certain salary, called your base. That's yours to keep and rely on. Above that the company gives you a commission according to a mutually agreed upon formula.

Salary: Some sales jobs pay a straight salary. These jobs almost always come with bonuses. If not, you can try to negotiate one.

Salary and Bonus: A bonus is a one-time payment of a fixed amount of money for achieving a certain level of sales. It could be a quarterly bonus, or a bonus that automatically kicks in when you reach your goal.

Residual Commission: This is a type of commission that keeps on paying even if you quit the company. In insurance sales, for instance, after you've been with the company for a certain length of time, you're entitled to commissions on the payments people make to the policies you sold them whether or not you work for the company any longer.

When your sales work involves a lot of new account generation, you would be wise to negotiate a residual commission on those new accounts. The thinking here is that the reward for *selling* the account belongs to you; after you leave and the account is *maintained,* a portion of the income should still be yours for a while.

Here's an interesting example of negotiating.

> A client of mine moved into the art sales field. She found a collection of valuable art that was being held in trust and was being stored for future sale. She wanted to be the agent to sell the paintings and didn't know how much to ask for in salary. This example is very illustrative of the "Make Me A Buck" principle. The paintings were a *cost* to the estate while in storage; by adding Liz they changed into a *profit.* Similarly, Liz without an art collection to market was just another Girl Friday. Both parties could win here. Now the question was: who would win how much?
>
> First we determined her value in the matter. We figured that the collection *as is* would sell for $200,000 to a big gallery. By arranging special exhibits, auctions, and gallery showings, she estimated she could bring in $500,000 over time. Therefore the difference between present and future sales is $300,000, the "value added" she could produce. If it took her two years or twenty to do this, the added value to be shared in some fashion between her and the estate would still be $300,000.
>
> However, this $300K is just an estimate (wild guess?). Who bears the burden of the risk that the whole venture might be a flop? If she were on straight commission, taking on all the risks of the venture, she could negotiate for 50-85 percent of the net increased value (that's roughly 30-50 percent of the gross sales price); if you take *all* the risk, you ought to get *most* of the reward. If the estate would pay her living expenses for six months, perhaps the compensation would be base plus a smaller commission on the sale.

Paintings increase in value as the artist becomes better known. If Liz got the paintings into the hands of collectors, she would be the ultimate reason for the increased value whether or not she was still actively marketing the works. Therefore, she could credibly negotiate for some residual commission on all works sold after she leaves.

Any salary could also be structured as a draw against commission. Since *her* risk is higher with a draw, *her* reward should be higher than on a base or salary. On the other hand, if the estate wanted to take on the risk, they could pay her a good salary for a year or two and call it even. She could also negotiate a salary with a bonus for a certain number of paintings sold within the year.

Then she could lay claim to some of the more elusive dollars: the *savings* generated as the storage costs decrease (FYI storing a painting is not like renting a U-Haul self storage locker—it's big bucks); the *interest* on the increased earnings as it comes in over two, three, or more years. On the other hand, the costs of transportation, taxes, gallery rental, and agent commissions should be figured into the deal if you wish to be fair.

You can see from this how compensation can be set up many different ways depending on what risk/reward ratio you're willing to accept. Also notice that you can negotiate individual parts of the package; you can significantly increase your *total* compensation package by changing or adding *one element.*

Performance Bonuses

For those who are not in sales, negotiating a performance bonus can be a very win/win way of negotiating extra income. Putting a bonus in your compensation package, based on the profitability of the area you are working in, gives you an incentive to work and your employer a way to make more money. Retail store managers, franchise operators, and department managers regularly get incentive bonuses based on target sales figures. You can negotiate your own version of this no matter what your job. Just pin a number to the quantity or quality of your work, using some objectively measurable criteria. Or pose an open-ended question to your employer, like: "Let's consider setting up a special bonus to encourage excellent performance. Can you think of a workable one?"

Two variations of the bonus are profit sharing and stock options. Stock options generally have been offered only to executives and the very upper levels of corporate management. That makes sense, because their decisions directly affect the value of their company in the marketplace, and that value determines the price of the company's stock. But recently stock options have become available to lower levels of management. Some of the most motivated and successful companies have what are known as employee stock ownership programs, or ESOPs.

While you would hardly be able to negotiate in a job interview for an entire ESOP for the company, you can suggest profit sharing if your work has a very direct bearing on the company's profits. Profit sharing can be computed monthly, quarterly, or yearly as a percentage of the organization's gross or net revenues. Your research can come into play here by giving you some sense of what's standard for the particular field and the level of position you are exploring.

Insurance

One benefit most companies offer is insurance. Insurance plans vary from company to company, and you should ask to see what the plan and the coverages are. You may wish to negotiate for a different deductible in your medical program. You can also ask about dental insurance, life insurance, and special medical expense provisions like disability pay. If you are unemployed and currently paying your own insurance premiums, you may negotiate to be covered by insurance right away rather than after the typical three-month waiting period.

While you're at it, double-check that the insurance you do get from the company will extend three months beyond your termination date in the event you should leave. Some states have legislation requiring six months' post-employment medical coverage. Legislation called COBRA requires that you be allowed, at your own expense, to remain on company health insurance at 101 percent of premium for up to a year after you leave. If you would like your employer to provide "X" months of coverage should you leave, ask for it now.

Cars and Expense Accounts

For positions where there is a lot of travel, discuss the travel and mileage allowance or the possibility of getting a company car. A company car may be worth several thousand dollars because it saves your paying insurance and maintenance costs on your own vehicle and depreciating that vehicle, and in certain cases may even save you all the taxes on those expenses.

Another benefit to clear up now is the expense account or entertainment account, especially if you are in sales. What do they consider customary expenses, and what exceptions are there?

Professional Memberships

If you have done your research for the position, you are probably aware of the professional association in your area of expertise. If you explain to the employer how a membership can help you be more productive for them, they should be willing to pay your membership dues and give you time off for meetings or training in your field.

Vacation and Personal Days

If you can't increase the money, perhaps you can reduce the time! Negotiate vacation, personal days, or your hours per week.

Let's get one thing clear on the vacation issue. No one *pays* you to go on vacation. You *earn* it. First, you earn it by doing extra work to help cover for others when they go on vacation. Second, you are only paid to bring in more money than you cost. You do not bring in money on vacation. So two weeks' vacation pay is really just fifty weeks of earnings spread out over fifty-two weeks. However, on vacation you do restore and replenish your energy (in theory, at least). Since that fresh energy can generate more profit, employers can sometimes be persuaded that extra vacation bennies will pay off for them.

First ask what their vacation, sick days, and personal days policies are. Then when you discuss vacation always frame it as a way to help you be more productive on the job. You might say, "I tend to throw myself so entirely into my work that I need a few breaks during the year; I'd like _____ weeks vacation."

See if you can get at least one more week than they offer—even if it's seven personal days scattered through the year. Or see if you can *earn* more vacation time or personal days by achieving 100 percent attendance over a given period of time. Many companies would love their employees to call in *well* and take a prearranged earned wellness day rather than to call in sick on short notice.

Relocation Expenses

Relocation expenses aren't always offered. They are generally part of a new compensation package whenever your present employer requests that you relocate. With a new employer, it is common only in executive positions, or whenever they want you badly enough.

Some relocation perks that you can calculate and might consider requesting are: company purchase of your present or future home and company payment of moving fees, closing costs, real estate broker's fee, early mortgage prepayment penalty, mortgage rate differentials, family transportation costs to look at new homes, appliance installation, and lodging fees while looking or waiting for a new home.

Others

Here's a list of some other things you might consider: Christmas bonuses; matching funds investment program; deferred salary; corporate gasoline from private pumps; free parking; corporate cafeteria or executive dining room privileges; pension plans (do you contribute or does the company pay in full?); severance pay; credit union; company-paid physical examinations; country club or health club memberships; and use of the corporate plane, boat, or vacation property.

Also ask about tuition reimbursement. Are there specific courses or degree work that would help you perform your job? Ask if they will pay, or help pay, some of those costs.

Still more bennies and perks are estate- or financial-planning assistance, tax and legal assistance, and corporate products discounts.

A list of Perquisites and Benefits appears in Figure 7-1.

I   BASIC COMPENSATION
  Base salary
  Sales commission
  Bonuses

II   BENEFITS
  Vacation time   Sick Days   "Wellness" days
  Insurance:
             Life   Medical   Dental   Disability
  C.O.L.A.

III PERQUISITES   Relocation:
  Profit sharing   moving expense
  Stock options   mortgage rate differential
  Legal assistance   mortgage prepayment
  Tuition reimbursement   penalty
  Annual physical exam   real estate brokerage
  Special training courses   closing costs
  Deferred compensation   trips for your family to look
  C.P.A. and tax assistance   for a home
  Financial planning assistance   lodging fees while between
  Pension plan   homes
  Mortgage funds   shipping of boats and pets
  Short term loans   installation of appliances,
  Child care   drapes, and carpets
  Country club membership   Matching investment program
  Luncheon club membership   (401K)
  Executive dining room   Company purchase of your home
     privileges   Company car or gas allowance
  Severance pay   Professional or trade association
  Office space, equipment   dues
  Future salary reviews   Athletic club membership
  Secretarial/Support staff   Consumer product discounts
  Starting date   Outplacement fees after
                                         termination
                                     Insurance benefits after
                                         termination (now generally
                                         mandated through COBRA)
                                     Overrides on others' performance
                                     Time/expenses of attending trade
                                     shows, and national conferences

Figure 7-1. NEGOTIATION CHECKLIST

Time to Think it Over

After you've discussed these areas, the offer should be pretty clear. You've worked hard, held your ground, and believed in yourself. Now comes the hard part:

DON'T TAKE THE JOB!!! (YET)

Money decisions are best made in the cool climate of logic and impartiality. Remember, you've been working toward this offer for months! You're eager and stimulated. It's new and exciting. But deciding in the heat of the moment makes for poor financial decisions. Anyone who compares their grocery bill when they went shopping with a hungry stomach to their bill when they went shopping with a full stomach will concur.

Give yourself time to think but don't be cool, indifferent, or undecided. When you've finished negotiating, put all your enthusiasm back in gear and say, "This sounds terrific! I think we've really got a solid match here. Would you jot all this down so we're clear, and I'll get back to you *as soon as you need to know*. When do you need to know?"

It is extremely important to maintain your enthusiastic voice, gestures, and energy so your request for time is not taken as a lack of interest in the job. There's a delicate line here between demanding time and requesting clarity.

One client lost an offer because instead of framing it as a request for clarity, he made it a demand: "I'll need time to think about this. I'll call you in a couple of days." "Well," the employer responded (they had been talking for weeks before this offer and negotiation), "if you're still undecided, we don't want you." The employer had interpreted his response as stalling or hesitation.

Put yourself in Ms. Employer's shoes. She has just concluded a long arduous process of finding the person who is going to finally solve her problems. She has struggled through nebulous and difficult negotiations with you and struck a deal. She is now eager to close the deal and the last thing she wants to hear is, "I'll think about it." (Especially since any salesperson will tell you "I'll think about it" is usually a polite way of saying "No.") On the other hand, you do need some time to make sure all the bases are covered.

How do you ask for it? Here are some more examples: "Yes! We're done! I can't wait to get started. I will need to look over this to make sure we haven't forgotten anything, so when do you want my final confirmation?"

Or: "OK, I'm giving my tentative 'yes' right now and I'll give you the permanent one as soon as you need to hear it. When would that be?" [answer] "OK, I don't see anything left to talk about right now. I'll sleep on this, look at it again to make sure we haven't missed anything, and confirm it in writing by that date."

Juggling Two or More Offers

What if you can't operate on their timetable? Suppose they want a decision in one week, and you have another offer pending that will take two weeks to mature? Then it's best to suggest your own time frame and see if they can work within it.

"This meets all my criteria for what I want," you say, "and I have every indication that this is the correct match, but I want to consider this very carefully. I would like two weeks to let this decision settle. Will that work with your schedule?"

Sometimes it will, sometimes it won't. The hardest part about job hunting is that offers generally come one at a time. You are seldom comparing one offer with another. Instead you're comparing a bird in the hand with two in the bush. The key in buying time to leverage other offers is to concentrate not so much on extending the firm offer as on accelerating the pending one.

If your second offer is of any strength at all, then you have a good relationship established already with the hiring individual (generally not the same as the personnel person). Use this rapport. Tackle the situation as a team. You will need to have a face-to-face meeting with this potential boss, explain the problem, and ask for assistance in solving it.

"I have another offer," you explain. "The job is not better than yours, or worse, just different. Frankly, my preference is to take the one in which I can make the best contribution. How can we get things moving here to meet the deadline of my first offer?"

If you have a good rapport, you can work together to accelerate

Juggling Two or More Offers.

things. If there's no interest in assisting you, that's a strong indication that the second offer is less of a fit than the first.

Sometimes, however, job 2 can't be hurried and job 1 can't be delayed. So if you're pressed to say yes or no to job 1 without having a yea or nay from employer 2, use your own judgment. You can:

Tell job 1 about job 2 and press for more time: "The reason I'd like that extra week is to get all the facts about another pending offer. Can we arrange it?"

Tell job 1 yes, but warn them that if job 2 comes up, you would have to consider accepting the other job and quitting theirs.

Tell job 1 yes, and cross the next bridge if and when you come to it. (You should be able to find a way to compensate employer 1 fairly for the month of training and the cost of hiring a replacement if you later pick job 2. If this is not your plan, then this option is not good human relations and will probably come back to haunt you.)

Tell job 1 yes and forget job 2.

Probably the best way to make the choice is to use your own internal measurement of which job would work best. Say yes to that one. Period. Even if it means losing the bird in the hand *and* the two in the bush. Your integrity and focus will soon line up job 4—maybe better than all its predecessors.

How do you decide which is best?

Examine the offers and give each of them grades A through F in these areas: satisfaction, professional growth, growth in responsibility, location, people/company style, and compensation. These are explained on the chart in Figure 7-2. Fill in the chart by writing down the grades and then numbering each area in order of importance: Priority 1 through 6.

Start with your highest priority, and compare the jobs point by point; you'll know which is the better offer.

If it's still too close to tell, then what are you waiting for? Tell job 1 yes and job 2 no!

Urgent Employers

Occasionally your prospective employer will ask you to decide right in the room. Whether you are juggling many offers or desperately clinging to one, you do not want to do this.

You've said, "I'll get back to you as soon as you need to know. When do you need to know?"

They say, "We need to have your answer right now."

You ask for clarification: "Fine, tell me about that."

They say, "Charlie's flying to London, Sharon's going on vacation, and we need someone aboard by Monday. We need to know right now."

This seems reasonable, so you work with it.

If you're at all interested, say "YES! This looks great! Right now I'm ready to accept, but I like to make my decisions carefully. I'm sure you would want careful decisions from me when I'm working for you. I can't see that anything would come up to change my mind, but if there's any way to get me some objective time to solidify my thinking on this I would appreciate it." If they want this to be an impulsive decision, you'll oblige. Say yes, and base it on your judgment of the moment. If something comes up before Monday, you'll call back and impulsively say no!

In any event, leave the negotiations open a little: "Decide now? Why, yes, of course! I accept! There may be a detail or two in the compensation package we've overlooked, so if I think of anything I'll let you know in the next couple of days."

Now, remember the phrase that was presented on a previous page: "Would you jot this all down?"

When to Get It in Writing

Having the employer jot the offer down is doubly important in hurry-up situations. Things are going fast, and you want to know that what you negotiated for will not get lost in the shuffle. Jotting it down is a way of getting your employer to perceive himself as making these commitments to you. As the saying goes, "A verbal contract isn't worth the paper it's printed on."

In a normal-paced situation, as long as you have agreed to a definite date for acceptance, there should be no danger of losing an offer to interlopers, and you can wait for a confirmation letter from the employer. If they should happen to renege, they probably weren't worth working for anyway.

Some normal-paced situations, though, also call for jotting it down. That includes any time there are special provisions, fees, expenses, or agreements. If the offer is more complicated than the standard one of salary, benefits, and starting date, you should get it in writing right off the bat. That doesn't mean it has to be formally typed on letterhead. Just jot it down neatly during the interview and ask your employer to look it over. Then have them make a duplicate for you and keep the original for themselves. You'll be glad you got it all clear and so will your employer.

Figure 7-2. Offer Comparison Chart

PRIORITY		GRADE	
		JOB 1	JOB 2
	Satisfaction		
	Opportunity to be doing work activities I		
_____	am skilled in and enjoy.	_____	_____
	Professional Growth		
	Opportunity to expand my skills and be-		
_____	come a better professional in my field.	_____	_____
	Growth in Responsibility		
	Opportunity to be promoted, or to expand		
	the job to take on higher level problems as I		
_____	master the present ones.	_____	_____
	Location		
	Commuting distance and geographic loca-		
_____	tion of the job. Amount of travel required.	_____	_____
	People/Company Style		
	Are they people I can work with? Is the		
	company managed in a style that will allow		
_____	me to be successful?	_____	_____
	Compensation		
_____	Wages, bennies, perks.	_____	_____

Whenever you have a *lot* at stake by accepting an offer—like resigning another position—you'll definitely want the offer in writing, and this time it should be typed out in a formal letter. Generally you'll have no problem getting that letter and, more importantly, a day to solidify your decision. Delay giving notice to your present employer until you have your letter from the new one.

The final acceptance of an offer can be done by phone. In the normal-paced version, you will take the time you need to think out the offer coolly and then call to accept. When you call you may request a more formal written offer so that you don't quit your present job and then find yourself unemployed. In larger companies the personnel department does this within a week, or you can offer to write a detailed letter of acceptance yourself, if you wish. In any event, communicate your enthusiasm once again, and assure your employer how well you expect this to work out.

What if you know the job is perfect and the package is super? *Why not* say yes right away? Well, besides depriving yourself of the objectivity you'd gain by waiting, it's a matter of style. As Eli Djeddah, a pioneer in career counseling, said, "It's simply not dignified." You want to be treated with respect when you begin your new job. If you wait before accepting the offer, you'll be respected for your clear-headed approach to things, and your employer's joy at their newborn employee will be all the more sweet for a day or so of pacing in the waiting room.

CHAPTER EIGHT

Special Situations

This chapter deals with some situations job seekers often encounter in their campaigns that may require special strategies or, in some cases, making exceptions to the salary-making rules. It also includes a "special consideration"—how to present a good image to employers.

Ads and Applications That Say "Salary History Required"

Some ads get pretty nosy about your salary requirements. However, even an ad that reads:

> Salary history required. Resumes without salary histories will be shredded into oblivion, and the applicant will be excommunicated *ipso facto*, held up to public scorn and opprobrium, fined, imprisoned, and in various and sundry ways maltreated . . .

should end, " . . . and hired if we think you can help us out of this mess."

Want ads have been described as "desperate screams for help emanating from somewhere deep in the corporate diaphragm." They are last resorts for people who need help so badly they pay dearly for an ad. I don't care how strongly an ad demands your numbers, you will not be passed over if you're right for the job and you show them respect.

Why do they want these figures? To screen, remember? They don't want to waste the time talking to you if they "can't afford" you in their **budget** stage. Your best approach to these ads is to acknowledge their need to screen, and stick to your principles about postponing money until there's a match.

So write in your cover letter something like, "I understand you've requested a salary history; I'm paid roughly the market-value of a (job

<u>title</u>) with _____ years experience, and while I'm not willing to publish my compensation package, I'd be happy to discuss it in an interview." Then in the interview say, "The level of responsibility looks right here, and since I'd be interested in fitting into your salary structure, I'm sure we can come to a good agreement. Let's discuss the job and match for the moment."

The same applies to an application form. When it asks for salary expectations, write "open." When it asks for previous salary history, leave it blank. If it says "Fill in every blank and answer every question," put "competitive" in the salary slot, with an asterisk and a note at the bottom saying, "*I'd be glad to discuss this personally in an interview." In the interview say, "I'd be glad to discuss it in a *hiring* interview. I don't think salary will be a problem. Let's see how I can help you."

Discussing Salary at Networking Interviews

During job interviews always follow salary-making rule 1: Never discuss salary until you've been offered the job. However, during nonjob interviews, salary discussions can sometimes be appropriate. Occasionally people will want to know your salary expectations as a way of understanding what level of work you want and are able to handle.

I instructed one client of mine to *begin* her networking interviews with a salary discussion. Since she was working for a temporary services agency, she could be mistaken for a $5-an-hour gofer unless she made her potential clear. She stated her conversations with a statement like, "I know I'm able to handle responsibilities that pay in the high twenties. I'm flexible about where I start, and I'm interested in talking with you to identify paths to that end."

This brings up the question about how to ask for salary information when you're *not* interviewing for a job.

In America discussing one's salary is practically taboo in social conversation. People are curious about "who's making what," but are too afraid to ask. So when you offer a you-tell-me-yours-and-I'll-tell-you-mine deal, it's too good to pass up. Even then you'll only be getting a range, with their salary situated anonymously in the middle.

People often attach identity, status, value, and prestige to their incomes, and revealing that can be scary—too intimate. I know counselors, lawyers, mechanics, and even baby-sitters who are too shy to ask colleagues what they charge per hour. Nevertheless, if you intend to add a networking approach to your job-hunting campaign, you will need to discuss salary with your contacts. It will probably feel awkward to discuss it and awkward to avoid it, but you need to discuss it.

Keep in mind again that your salary is linked to your level of responsibility, so you need to treat salary as a thermometer: You'll be telling people how much "heat" you can take. Before you seriously talk to people on a job hunt, do the print research in the library as described in Chapter 5. Look at the jobs and ask yourself which ones you realistically think you could handle. Get the range by looking it up or ordering a personalized pay comparison. Then let people know that range so that you can do a reality check on your expectations.

Phrasing it in terms of responsibilities you can handle might sound like: "What would be the biggest challenges you could see me handling? And what would positions like that pay?"

Another research question you can ask a contact is, "With the level of experience you see in me, and considering the functions I can handle, what would you estimate my salary range in this field to be?" And you can follow up with, "Well, I've researched (<u>supervisor</u>) positions in the (<u>travel</u>) industry, (<u>production supervisor</u>) positions in (<u>light manufacturing</u>), and a few other types of positions, and I come up with a range of _____ to _____. What would I have to do in your field to get that kind of money?"

You can, if you like, go first in this situation. As long as you aren't discussing a specific job opening, it is an open-ended conversation and not likely to box you in. This is especially true if you are talking about your researched estimate. Remember, too, that they may not really know. You probably realize by now that since people would sooner discuss their sex lives and last session with their psychiatrist than reveal their salary, their estimates of your earning abilities may really be a blind guess. Your own estimates may educate *them* on the size of the problems you want to handle; with that clarity, you'll get better-quality referrals to other contacts.

Special Considerations: Image and Presentation

Know that part of getting top dollar is your self-presentation. If your own estimate of value and competence is not matched by your contacts' estimates, the problem could be your image or communication.

No matter how terrific you are on the inside, you must express it or it will remain buried. Thomas Gray, in his *Elegy Written in a Country Churchyard*, pondered how a "mute inglorious Milton" might be buried there because he never expressed his capabilities:

> *Full many a gem of purest ray serene,*
> *The dark unfathom'd caves of ocean bear:*
> *Full many a flower is born to blush unseen,*
> *And waste its sweetness on the desert air.*

Your light will do you no good hidden under a bushel basket. Getting what you're worth means showing it! It means dressing in your salary range, displaying etiquette in your salary range, grooming in your salary range, and speaking in your salary range. There are studies that show the most reliable indicator of a person's salary level is his or her vocabulary, and that a limp, fishy handshake could cost you thousands of dollars.

Look around you and notice the way your target-level people dress and act. Imitate them or their superiors. A client of mine heeded my advice and dressed in a well-fitting, moderately priced suit when the position he was interviewing for was very short-sleeves. The business owner who interviewed him told him he was over-qualified for that position, but he'd been thinking of another position that would be more in his line. Investment: one suit $250; Return: 1200 percent—one job $3,000 better than the original.

Besides looking the part, you also need to communicate your capabilities in a strong, positive way that is directly understandable and applicable to your prospective employer's needs. It's common sense: The stronger you construct the match and compatibility, the more **fudgit** and **judgit** you'll engender. Being a job and career consultant, of course, I recommend *minimally* consulting a candid friend for a critique of your self-presentation. And if you *really* want the best return from your efforts, hire a coach: a career consultant whose reputation you've researched. Besides saving you time (which equals money) in your job hunt, and focusing you on your best market possibilities, a coach can really train you to sell yourself at the top of your potential.

"Overqualified"

My well-dressed client (above) evoked a constructive "overqualified" response. What if *overqualified* is negative? I had a less-fortunate client who applied for two almost identical positions in two very similar companies. One told him he couldn't handle the job, while the other told him he was overqualified! It's a very subjective term that can mean different things.

Overqualified relates to salary negotiations one time out of three. It means your potential employer is worried that:

You'll be bored, so bored that you'll last a few months and then quit for more exciting work.

You'll be expensive, so expensive that you'll work a few months and then quit for better-paying work.

You're a creep, such a creep that in a few days you'll alienate everybody and get fired.

The first is a focus issue; the second a salary issue; the third, well, in Fritz Perls' words, " . . . if we meet it's beautiful. If not, it can't be helped."

The first means the job really isn't for you! Unless you're interested in starting in the cellar and working your way up, you should refocus the interview on where the company might have challenges at your level.

The second is really a variation on salary-making rule 1. If you're being judged as too expensive, you're really discussing salary before the offer. Although it's still too early to discuss numbers, you should bring up and face this issue head on. A variation of "I'm sure we can come to a good salary agreement" works well. Or try "Overqualified? I'm glad you brought that up, because I want a job that will work out well for a long time. So far this seems like the right kind of challenge for me. If salary is an issue, I'm sure we can handle that if the job is right." Or simply "Overqualified? Maybe you're worrying that you can't pay me enough and I'd leave. Don't! If the job is right and the money fair, I'll be satisfied."

Again you must know yourself and the job well enough. If it really is below your capabilities and you see no potential to expand the duties, then you *are* overqualified and shouldn't be interviewing there in the first place.

Dealing With Recruiters and Employment Agencies: Intermediaries

What if you sign up with employment agencies, which tend to place support staff, or recruiters, who work with top professionals and executives? What do you tell them when they ask about salary?

Both types of intermediaries are exceptions. You *may* discuss salary expectations first. They need to know your salary requirements legitimately, to screen you. If you recall, the purpose of postponing salary discussion is to give you time to move the employer from **budget** to **fudgit** to **judgit**. When you're dealing with an intermediary, you have access only to the **budget** stage. That's because, at least initially, only the intermediary has contact with the employer. So when dealing with recruiters, let them know your current earnings and requirements—especially the salary that represents the level of challenge you can handle.

The same goes for employment agencies. Instead of holding back your expectations, sometimes you'll have to be *doubly* clear about what salary you will and won't accept, or you'll be running all over town talking to people about low-paying jobs. Throughout the rest of this section. I'll refer to the intermediary as the "recruiter." However, the same principles hold true for employment agents.

When asked about their current earnings, some people are tempted to inflate them. Never do this. There are three sound reasons why I recommend 100 percent truth in stating your salary information: **1.** Frank money talk with a recruiter shows integrity and good faith. **2.** Recruiters can often sense when you are fabricating your earnings, and they're trained in effective methods of getting at the truth which include verifying with previous employers. This is a service the client employer expects and is paying for. **3.** Experienced recruiters are excellent judges of value, so salary history will not prejudice them, and you can still establish your value with facts about your performance potential.

Even though you'll lack contact with the employer at the start, experienced recruiters are generally pretty accomplished at moving an employer from **budget** to **judgit** themselves. Since the fee they earn for a placement (believe me, they earn it) usually depends on the first year's salary, they'll try to get you the highest offer possible. On the other hand, since they're only paid on placement, just getting you hired is their first priority. Your salary is secondary. If the employer "can't afford you," the recruiter will look for another candidate. [Job-hunting tip: In this case, ask the recruiter if there are other client companies who might want your talents. If you are a very strong candidate, some recruiters will market you to their client base to earn extra fees. It is the exception, not the rule, but you've got nothing to lose!]

Paradoxically the recruiter's concern for just getting you hired, which can "budget" you out, can also motivate them to "bend" the budget for you. Why? Because they want a compensation package attractive enough to make you say yes!

Recruiters usually at least try to extend the offer on the company's behalf. Before they present it, they make every effort to clear all aspects of it with the hiring person. That includes dollars, incentives, benefits, perks, relocating expenses, sign-on bonuses, and others. Sometimes recruiters negotiate the offer; more often, however, they have no authority to spend their clients' money, so this is precisely the time they bow out. Often, then, the candidate is able to negotiate the offer directly with the employer during the interview. All you'll need to know is who is actually handling the negotiations in your case.

Will your recruiter spill the beans and hurt your negotiating position with the employer? Well, recruiters invariably tell the employer your current or past earnings, when asked. However, if the candidate earns more than the budgeted salary, but the employer may go higher, the recruiter may withhold the candidate's earnings information until the employer has interviewed that person. I know a recruiter who got a candidate $30,000 more that way.

Often, however, the employer is firm about the highest potential offer. If that looks like a problem, the recruiter will avoid putting any more time into what might be an unworkable situation, by asking the candidate if the offer is okay. If that happens to you, you *may* choose to interview anyway, especially if you're unemployed or the opportunity looks especially good.

However, you should know that an experienced recruiter won't send out on an interview candidates who:

Are motivated to look at a new position because of money only;

Won't reveal their earnings or have been found to have exaggerated them;

Will entertain a counteroffer from their current employer;

Have unrealistic expectations about the salary or job they'll accept.

During your interview with the employer, the "establish value before price" rule remains in effect, although you approach it differently. Since recruiters are obliged to reveal your past or current earnings when asked (after all, the employer pays the fee), it doesn't matter if you tell the employer too. Your recruiter should actually suggest that you do. The recruiter will also, hopefully, show you how to sell your worth.

When the employer asks "What salary are you looking for?" you can say: "I'm sure if you could double your current earnings with the right job, you'd jump at the chance, wouldn't you? So would I! But realistically, I'm earning $_____ now, and I hope that an offer would be somewhere between that and twice that figure, based on your recognition of my true worth to your organization." Or, "When the recruiter described your company and opportunity, she explained that your firm was very competitive with the market and that you typically hired top talent as a result. That assures me that when you make me an offer, it will be both fair and attractive."

Candidates who report their earnings to the dollar without prompting get high marks for honesty, and everything else they say about their background becomes easier to accept. So go ahead and give both the recruiter and the employer your exact salary, but make it very clear *what range* you think you're qualified for.

Salary Boxes

Sometimes you'll be negotiating with a company where the compensation is all figured out ahead of time. Perhaps they've implemented the

Hay System, or the ranges have been set by law—public sector positions are often like that—and you fit into a category. Teaching positions are systematically boxed into academic degrees and years of experience. Each box has its own salary attached. The federal government has grades, and steps within the grades; positions are assigned a rating of G.S.8, G.S.9, and so on, and a standard salary.

You *can* negotiate these, although it's harder. If you can't change the salary attached to the box, perhaps you can change the box. Doesn't your volunteer work with Great Books and your adult education classwork really add up to another year of teaching experience? Perhaps your two years in that inner-city school are equivalent to three or four years of normal teaching. (It took several years off your life! That's for sure.)

The other strategy to use is reassigning the grade itself. The earlier in the formation stages a job is, the easier this is to do. If the job has been classified as G.S.5 for years and years, it's unlikely you can make a case for upgrading it, unless you can negotiate adding some responsibilities to it. But if it's a new position, you might be able to show how it really should be upgraded.

A client of mine was told in the interviewing process that this particular company's policy was to give all the information about degree, experience, project assignment, etc., to the personnel department, and they would come up with an offer. That was it! He could only "take it or leave it" once it was figured out! Sound nonnegotiable? Well, we found a way for him to make the right noises to the right ears about his value and about the importance of getting the compensation figured out attractively. While we couldn't change the final number, we influenced beforehand the people who made up that number. When the offer came in, it was a 100-percent salary increase over his present job.

Another client interviewed to teach at a public high school. Three times during the interview the principal said, "You understand that this is an eight-tenths position, don't you?" That means it was a four-day-a-week job at four-fifths (eight-tenths) the full-time salary.

"Well," my client replied, "I understand that it's an eight-tenths position, and if I'm the one you want I'm sure we can find a way to work out fair compensation."

Turns out my client *was* the one they wanted, but eight-tenths of the salary box was too low for him to accept. So first he tried to get eight-tenths of a different box. Would the principal consider his master's degree the equivalent of "master's plus fifteen hours"? After all, it had required thirty more credit hours than other teachers' master's degrees.

"Sorry, no," the principal responded.

Then how about credit for an extra year of experience, since his master's internship had been a very demanding full-time position for six months with delinquent kids?

"No, any exceptions would bring on grievances from the teachers' union."

Well, how about special assignments like debating coach, or audiovisual coordinator?

"Aha! We could arrange that, yes! Mr. Smith has been complaining about the audiovisual duties and would love to hand them over to someone else."

Result: eight-tenths position + a few hours audiovisual coordinating = a total salary 10 percent *higher* than a *full-time* position in that box. Another interesting thing is that six people had interviewed for and *rejected* the position when they learned it was only eight-tenths.

The moral is that when interviewers say "inflexible" or "nonnegotiable," they're still in the **budget** stage. So wait for **judgit**, and look for ways to change either the box you fit in, the box the job fits in, or the box makers' minds!

Over the Phone

Final acceptance of an offer can be handled by phone, but whenever possible avoid doing the initial negotiating that way. If you are given an offer over the phone, tell the individual that it sounds very workable, and since it is important that the agreement be clear and good for both parties, you'd like to stop in and talk it over in detail. You will have a better opportunity to get a fully negotiated deal when you and your potential employer are giving it your full attention, which you can't do on the phone.

When it's not possible to stop in, you can make sure you and the employer are undisturbed and negotiate as you would face-to-face by simply setting a time to call back to handle it. Otherwise you're off guard, caught in the middle of something. Call back at a time when you can concentrate on negotiating.

Delayed Negotiations

Another special area to note is over-delayed salary discussions. You know from salary-making rule 1 to wait for a job offer before discussing salary, but don't wait longer than that. If you get a hiring signal from an employer and they don't bring up salary, you bring it up.

You could say, "Well, I guess that means we better make a deal. What did you have in mind?"

Letting it go beyond offer time could mean your employer plans to hire you without negotiating and assumes you'll take what you get. Or else they're embarrassed.

I had a client who had every indication that the director of engineering wanted to hire him. The director had said, "You're just the person we're looking for."

"What was their offer?" I asked.

"Oh, we haven't talked money yet."

Uh oh!

He quickly followed my instructions to get right back on the phone, ask how firm their decision was, and suggest that they talk about salary. He was told, "Well, we'd love to have you, but you wouldn't take $28,000, would you?"

"Well, I'd consider it," he replied. "When can we talk, and who makes those decisions?"

He was hired two weeks later at a grade higher than the opening was originally rated. He made an extra $3,500 a year because he negotiated for his market value and fuller responsibilities. If he had waited, they would have been too shy to tell him they couldn't afford him, and he'd have lost the offer. He had to educate the man *inside* the company about the flexibility of salaries.

Remember, they may not know what you know: that money can be fudged to fit the person.

No Experience

How do you determine your value if you think you're inexperienced?

The first such people who come to mind are recent college graduates. I read a survey of Harvard MBA graduates a while ago, and their biggest worry was that they didn't have any experience that would attract an employer.

Other "I don't have any experience" people are career changers, foreign immigrants, high school students, even COBOL programmers switching to FORTRAN.

Please be careful! Your tendency is to be so glad that someone is offering you a job, that you accept whatever they offer with a beggar's nod and smile. Ponder the following points.

If you followed salary-making rules 1, 2, and 3, they're choosing *you*, not your price. They *really* want to hire you! They think you'll make or save them money!

You must have the ability to do the work, or they wouldn't be making you an offer.

Their hiring decision is 95-percent based on your personality, enthusiasm, and transferable skills. Only 5 percent has to do with your specialized knowledge. Since they *can't* teach manners and common sense, they hire it. Since they *can* teach their subject, they train you. Therefore, 95 percent of you *is* experience worth bargaining about.

This is it! This is the only time you'll be at the starting line. Here's your chance to begin the virtuous cycle of Ms. Worth.

What have you got to lose?

So if you think you have "no experience, remember the qualities that make you successful. To an offer of $X you'll say, "From my research, X is around entry level for salary. Considering my enthusiasm and my general success in the things I set out to do, I believe I'm worth midrange, say $Y. What can you do in that area?"

Summary of Special Situation Rules

When discussing salary expectations outside job interviews, focus on a researched level of responsibility and concomitant pay. With recruiters and employment agents, even when you're discussing a specific job, you may go first; stress your researched expectations, not your present salary, and give a wide range. Use this researched range, too, when confronted with rigid salary structures. See if you can get a new salary *within* that structure, basing it on your market value. When you're getting "over-qualified" feedback, or hesitancy in bringing up salary, check on the job offer status and initiate salary discussions. When you think you haven't any experience, choose to start Ms. Worth's virtuous cycle.

CHAPTER NINE

Raises & Salary Reviews

Why Would Your Boss Give You a Raise?

If you want a higher salary for your present job, it behooves you to answer this question: Why would anybody want to give somebody a raise?

By "raise," I don't mean a cost-of-living adjustment (COLA) to keep pace with inflation. If you've read the COLA section in Chapter 7, you realize that's no raise. Consumer prices have climbed so rapidly in recent years that most workers' "raises" have, in reality, just helped them keep up. For 1980, inflation was 13 percent, while for the next four years it was 11 percent, 5 percent, 7 percent, and 5 percent. That totals 41 percent by simple addition. But it's really more than that because inflation, like interest in savings accounts, compounds. So for 1980-85, inflation actually cut purchasing power almost 50 percent! For example, if you earned $20,000 in 1980 and $30,000 in 1985, you didn't receive a raise at all. You've had to earn one and a half times your 1980 salary just to maintain the same buying power.

But wait. It's even worse than that! In 1980 your income tax was withheld in the twenty grand bracket. Now you're paying taxes on thirty grand. So we're talking a 50- to 80-percent increase over five years just to buy the same home, clothes, and food as before.

If inflation is this huge, why would anybody want to give somebody a raise, too?

The answer is that employers don't *give* raises, employees *earn* them. Remember the "Make me a buck" principle? This is a corollary. The longer you are in a particular job, the better you perform it (hopefully). The better you perform it, the more goods and services you produce in that same forty-hour week. So since you're making the employer more bucks, a raise is just your fair share of those bigger profits.

Employers don't *give* raises. Employees *earn* them.

If you've been thinking you deserve a raise just because you reported to work all 251 days last year, you're mistaken. People act like they're *entitled* to a raise every year, but from your employer's perspective, continued raises without continued increases in productivity merely make you a prime target for the next layoffs. During the last recession, this happened to many managers who were being overpaid for the amount of work they did. They were either let go or encouraged to retire.

Earning It

At first glance, boosting your output might look like an overwhelming task. You may wonder just how much more productive you'd have to be to earn a raise. Say you're in the same job for ten years and you need to accomplish more each year, you might reach a point where you think, "I can't do any more than I'm already doing!"

But that's not so. If you set your sights correctly, you can contribute more every single year than the year before. I'm not talking about working harder, I'm talking about working *smarter*. If you put your brain to it, you can actually work less and accomplish more—and there are no upper limits. Especially in the nineties, when there are countless ways that electronics can "chip away" at many of the time-consuming tasks of yesteryear. And there's never an end to the level of satisfaction and commitment you can create in coworkers, management, customers, and vendors.

While you do need to be more valuable, you don't need to double your output to net a 5-percent raise. A solid record of good work is all that's required. If your mind is active and engaged in your job, productivity increases will happen automatically. All you need to do is notice them.

Since the focus of this book is salary and raise negotiating, this chapter will concentrate on *negotiating* raises you've earned, rather than *earning* raises to negotiate. The latter—performing on the job in such a way that you deserve a raise—is a book in itself. Two books, in fact:

Working and Liking It
Richard Germann, New York: Ballantine Books, 1984.

Get a Raise in 60 Days
Steve Kravette, New York: Bantam, 1983.

Richard Germann's book takes you through a program to create your ideal job out of your present one. It covers analyzing your best talents, establishing a contact/information network within your company, defining your ideal situation, gaining recognition for your worth, and launching a step-by-step campaign using research, communication, and persuasion.

Steve Kravette's book teaches you the attitude and level of performance you need to get a raise anytime you want one, without working overtime or changing company policies.

Both are powerful books, and I recommend them for strategies on earning a promotion or raise.

Communication Is the Key

Now we'll learn how to *negotiate*. Let's assume you've kept your shoulder to the wheel all year long. You have thrown every morsel of energy, creativity, and positive mental attitude humanly possible into your job. You have made them a bundle! How do you negotiate a raise?

Communication.

Specifically, communication in three steps:

1. Document your results.

2. Get your boss to acknowledge them.

3. Negotiate a raise the same way you'd negotiate a salary.

According to the saying, "Squeaky wheels get the grease," complainers may get more notice than you do. Don't assume that your boss knows what a good job you've done to keep things running so smoothly. If you have a boss who allows you the freedom to do a good job, and you've made things run efficiently, they're *less* likely to be aware of your accomplishments! They are so trusting of your work that they naturally pay attention to their own problems instead of your performance. They aren't motivated to delve into your accomplishments. Therefore you'll have to do it for them.

The best way is by keeping a job journal. If your review is due soon, start your journal by reviewing the period since your last raise, writing down the most significant things you've done. If your review is a ways off, begin your journal today and it will be your magic carpet to Raise-land later. Start by purchasing a spiral notebook big enough to hold large entries and small enough to tuck in a very accessible place.

I'm indebted to Carl Armbruster for the following description of a job journal, which is a splendid tool for negotiating raises.

A journal can assist your career in a number of ways, but none of them are magical. You have to work at career advancement, and the journal gives you excellent material to accomplish the task.

What do you write in your career log? There are four kinds of observations, and the first are observations about your achievements. As you work you are solving certain problems, learning new techniques, creating new approaches. Record these small triumphs in your journal, with enough factual information to describe exactly what happened and what the results were.

Quantifiable data is especially desirable, such as ballpark percentages, rounded dollar figures, or units of time. Achievements don't have to be earth-shaking (you weren't hired as a miracle worker), but they should be tangible evidence of your performance on the job.

The second set of observations comes from time spent studying your superiors, colleagues, subordinates, or customers. Start a policy of observing people in order to find out what their strongest talents are. Don't look for weaknesses and chinks in the armor, because negative appraisals don't lead anywhere. They just sour you on the people.

But a positive observation of what their skills are can help you respect them and thus lay a firm foundation for building good human relations. Also, you will know more precisely how to approach them effectively to get their support for your projects, promotions, or raises. Your notebook forces you to be aware of them.

The third set of observations includes your ideas for progress. How often have you had the experience of getting a brilliant insight into how to do your job better or create something more efficient and then two weeks later being unable to recall the idea that originally excited you so much? Insights of genius should be recorded since they may be lost due to the frailty of human memory.

The fourth kind of observation includes news items, information, or sources of information about your chosen career field, such as newspaper and magazine articles. You want to be a professional, to keep up with what's going on. Your reading in your field should be documented for future use.

Using a Job Journal

Use your journal in Step 1 of negotiating a raise: documenting your results.

A few weeks before your review, look through (or if you don't have a journal yet, think through) the first kind of observations: your achievements since your last raise. Especially note the differences between what you're doing now and what you did when you started at your last salary level. Measure your achievements in terms of dollars, people, productivity, exposure, or anything else countable or measurable.

Analyzing your work in terms of measurable results gives you a concrete success agenda to share with your raise-giver and shows you how you've actually been spending the time that, in effect, the employer buys from you.

In analyzing your results, take the raise-giver's viewpoint. What matters to them? What puts more money in their paycheck or bonus? What will they be able to parlay into their own raise or promotion? What do they care deeply about?

For example, you were tired of being bugged repeatedly about the same old tripe by every new employee. So you organized a training program for the new people who come into your department. As a result these people now know what they're doing. But what counts to your boss? The boss is interested that your training program cut 50 percent off the time he previously "wasted" on getting recruits up to speed. *And* that you were able to give 50 percent more of your own time to other money-making work because you didn't have to answer ridiculous questions every ten minutes.

This is where the second set of observations comes into play. Read through (or think about) what matters to your boss. These aren't always related to money. Bosses can also care about neatness, safety, morale, confidentiality, corporate visibility, efficiency, creativity, good press, or even fancy titles or time for golf. Knowing what your boss values will help you measure your results in language he or she will understand and appreciate. If you don't know what your boss considers important, ask!

Then take time to fill out pages something like the Review Preparation Worksheet in Figure 9-1.

Use a separate page for each achievement you've had since your last salary increase.

Then come up with goals for yourself for the next year. You can use the ideas section from your journal. Just as an example, say your idea is to start up a chocolate ice cream break at 10 a.m. each morning. If you have a chocoholic boss, you're fine. Otherwise project how much more work will get done, in the short or long term, so the discussion will have some merit.

Observations from the fourth section of your journal—news in your field—may also generate goals.

The Pre-review Memo

When you've assembled this material, put together a pre-review memo. Communication Step 2, you'll recall, is to get your boss to ac-

Achievement:

_____

_____

_____

_____

Results (be specific: money made or saved, time saved, percent improvement, and so on):

_____

_____

_____

_____

_____

_____

What value these results have to my boss (why the boss would care about them):

_____

_____

_____

_____

_____

_____

New problems/goals arising from this solution:

_____

_____

_____

_____

_____

Figure 9-1. Review Preparation Worksheet

knowledge your achievements. This can only come out of a personal
meeting; just sending the memo will do precious little. But *do* send the
memo. Make it one page. You can have a multi-page document for
backup purposes, but a one pager has a simple, unique advantage over a
longer version: Your boss will actually read it!

Start the memo by thanking your boss for the opportunity to work and contribute to the organization over the past _____ months or year. Since your review is coming up, you continue, you've prepared a summary of the highlights during that period, which you expect will lead to a conversation about the next _____ months' or year's goals. Then, in bulleted form, list your top five areas of achievement. Make them brief, positive, and results oriented.

Each area will correspond to one of three types: "Good Show," "Nice Going," or "Could've Been Worse."

"Good Show" is work you've done that directly affected the quality of products or services, or the quantity of profit or services. For example, "Solidified the communications with the independent distributors in Midwest region through personal visits and follow-up telephone work. Results: sales increased 37 percent over last year and distributor turnover reduced 20 percent."

In contrast to the measurable increases of "Good Show," "Nice Going" focuses on your ability to handle the routine stuff. Don't take the ordinary responsibilities of your job for granted. Remind your boss of the benefits that come from your just doing your job right. For example, "Oversaw word-processing unit, hiring and training sixteen operators over the past year, and maintaining the supplies and equipment. Results: You [the boss] have had, I believe, a completely worry-free year with regard to word processing, and no complaints of any substance from the staff."

The last category, "Could've Been Worse," notes what at first you might regard as failures. For example, "Lost three major clients," "Produced 30 percent fewer parts," "Turnover doubled," "Profits declined," or "We're really in debt now!" However, if you've been working hard, there is probably a case for "Things Could've Been Worse." Mention the circumstances under which you were working (careful—no blaming, just facts), and turn it into an accomplishment. For example, "Kept 50 percent of my staff during the past year despite salary reductions and layoffs. I have a committed group who will dedicate themselves to the company's effort to survive this recession and will keep your division going strong and ready for the next steps."

End the memo with a comment about how you look forward to a productive discussion. Do not mention raises in the memo.

Send the memo seven to ten days before your review.

To whom do you send it? The way this particular memo is constructed, it goes only to your reviewer. If you are far enough ahead of schedule (a month or so), you can take some of the same journal material and send it as a report to several managers. The purpose, of course, is to let people know about your good work, but the best way to do this is to make it a request for feedback. Prepare the one-page memo/summary, and include backup pages with some details on how you achieved your results, and an honest presentation of questions that occurred to you while you prepared the material. Nothing in life is so cut and dried that there aren't a few other options, a few worries about consequences, or a set of other considerations in our decision making. Getting other people's input on our decisions, albeit hindsight, is a way to be even more productive in the future. So send it out and invite discussion. Follow it up in a week on your own. Remember, if you do your work so well that nobody notices, nobody will!

Here's a case history of successfully sending a pre-review memo to several managers:

Jack was in charge of preventive maintenance at a medium-sized plant that manufactured tin cans. He did a great job. But until he documented his results, he didn't know how great.

By looking up the production records for the years before he was hired, Jack discovered how much money had been spent on repairs and how much had been lost due to production line downtime.

He listed the new procedures he'd put into place: methods for machine maintenance, critical-wear-testing of parts, and gathering input from production line employees. He documented several of the improvements and tagged each with an estimated dollar savings. They totaled an astounding $200,000!

Jack decided that since he'd been unaware of the extent of his contribution, his bosses must be doubly unaware. And since preventive maintenance means "doing things so nothing breaks," Jack was in exactly the kind of "Success is when nobody notices anything" position that further guarantees that higher-ups are oblivious to one's work.

During his first year he did have to cope with breakdowns, malfunctions, and downtime, but these were a carryover from his predecessor's shoddy work. His program's effectiveness wouldn't really show up until the next year!

His memo listed "Good Show" for improvements in the equipment and efficiency of operations, and the retrofitting of a machine that would have cost $80,000 to replace.

"Nice Going" included his record of the past six months, such as recording and analyzing data about when and how things broke, and initiating the "This machine is sounding strange" reports from the line that would pay off by catching things *before* they broke.

He had a "Could've Been Worse" on a breakdown that stopped production for eight hours. He pointed out that he was able to cut the normal sixteen-hour repair time in half.

Jack sent the report to several people in a *sincere* effort to gather even more ideas and suggestions. He got them. One was a terrific idea about rewards for employees who find potential trouble spots, which served as fodder for the next year's review.

Jack and I discussed the $200,000 in savings. We noted that this was pure profit, the equivalent of earnings generated by 2 to 4 million dollars in sales.

In Jack's case, management actually came to him and gave him an increase plus bonuses equal to a 50-percent raise. Of course, the boss doesn't always step forward like that, so let's get back to you.

At the Negotiating Table

For your review, make sure you have undisturbed time to go over your memo with the boss. Bring your own copy. Begin the discussion by going over your contributions. You'll either hear the boss acknowledge your effectiveness, or you'll have to ask for it. One way or another, get the boss to agree that you are effective! Otherwise you'll have earned a raise in deeds, but not in the place that counts: the boss's mind.

Then get the boss in line with your goals, to see if the ideas you've hatched fit into his or her plans. This discussion will happen pretty naturally. But at the end, request some clarity about whether the boss *wants* you to do these things. Be direct. Ask, "Are these goals important to you, and should I work on them?" Or, "How would you rank these in order of importance? Should I start on number 1 first?"

Now, as in salary negotiating, you've coaxed your employer as close to the **judgit** stage as possible. Therefore, as in salary negotiating, you *let the boss name the figure first.*

You may, if you wish, first educate them on the difference between a raise and a COLA. You still won't be naming a figure first, but you'll be indirectly stating that you expect your increase to do more than just keep pace with inflation. You could say, "Cost-of-living adjustment this year would be [5 percent], so I'd like to discuss what my raise will be."

As in salary negotiating you absolutely *must* know the market value for comparable positions. Your ability to strike a bargain at the top of the range depends on it. In a salary negotiation, the question of disclosing your present or past salary is important. In a raise negotiation that point is moot; obviously, your boss already knows your present salary. Therefore the most important thing is knowing your market value. You acquire that knowledge by researching two types of sources: external and internal. Use the other resources described in Chapter 5 to come up with a market value externally. Internally, make sure you nose around and find out whatever you can about compensation policies and practices and the current profitability and operating budget of your division, company, or organization. This will be useful for comparing your salary with others outside the company.

It's tempting to use your market knowledge and documentation of your value to come up with a figure and go first. Don't. You may think that declaring a value 20 percent above your present compensation will prompt them to budge their 2-percent plans, and it probably would. But if they intended to *double* your salary, do you think they'd go that high knowing you'd be tickled with less? Let them sweat. If you've made the best case for your value, quote Elwood P. Dowd, and say, "What did you have in mind?"

When you hear 2 percent, repeat it, wait 30 seconds looking glum, and respond by reporting your research. "I've spent some time looking into the current market value of this type of position," you say, "and my research indicates a range from $X to $Y. I'm not sure if you were aware of that. Considering my contributions that we've just discussed, I think a fair salary would be in the $Y range." If the boss seems skeptical, you could present documentation of your research, like a personalized pay comparison.

Remember, too, that fringes can easily compensate if your employer can't move the base. An extra week of vacation, for example, is a 2-percent raise. Look over the list of bennies and perks in Figure 7-1. Figure out which ones you could ask for, and ask.

From this point on you're on your own. Come up with a salary that is fair and will keep you committed and productive.

Creating Raises and Promotions

Don't just wait for reviews and anniversaries to ask for a raise, either! An ideal time to get an increase is when changes occur at work. When you do a tremendous job on a revenue-producing project, when you take on more work because someone quits and the position isn't filled—any time your value to the organization increases—take the opportunity to send a brief memo to your boss and discuss compensation. You may negotiate a one-time bonus, a raise, or, when your job changes significantly, something besides a raise (which is usually based on your last salary): a *new* salary appropriate to your *new* job.

Sometimes a new job just creeps up on you. When you document your accomplishments, notice how your job has evolved. Have you begun making decisions only the boss made before? Did the part-time help you hired to handle the rush turn into a full-time staff of one and a half people you now train and supervise? Are you now selling to customers you previously only serviced?

Do some subtraction. This year's responsibilities minus last year's responsibilities may yield a *big* remainder. It's called a new job. Instead of a raise, it deserves a whole new salary based on its actual value to the company.

Naturally, most employers will continue seeing you as your old self. So you're going to have to educate them about your new position. Otherwise they'll think that the jump from $20,000 to $30,000 a year is a 50-percent raise, when actually it's a new salary appropriate to your new job.

The *clearest* way to break the box your employer thinks you're in is to invent a new job title! For example, it'll be easier to get an "accounting services coordinator's" salary than an "accounting clerk's" raise. Don't, however, *call* it a promotion. Promotions sometimes have to be reviewed and approved. Yours has already occurred, and it's just as real as a formal promotion, so don't buy the line "We'll see if we can promote you."

You say, "I don't care about a title as much as simply being paid market value for the work I contribute here."

Now you've *negotiated* a raise, or even a promotion; you're feeling proud of yourself.

I can tell you from experience with many clients that this will definitely start you on the virtuous cycle of Ms. Worth. You'll win, your employer will win, and your future will be even brighter.

CHAPTER TEN

The "You Go First" Perspective

This book would not be complete without two discussions concerning the "you go first" method. One comments on the strategy for "you go first" that you may have read elsewhere; the other focuses on the worry most likely to get you to take the easy way out: "What if they get mad at me?"

The "You Go First" Strategy

Several authorities suggest that you go first. They often refer to the advice of John Crystal, a sage and pioneer in the field of job and career counseling.

Among several negotiating routes, Crystal suggests a strategy based on the existing salaries of your intended boss and your intended subordinates. Typically you will be earning less than your boss and more than your hirelings. So he suggests you research the salaries of those people. Say you come up with a spread like:

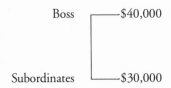

You would guess the range for your position would be $32,000 to $38,000. So to push your dollars to the top of the range, you would bracket the high end and be prepared to discuss salary at any time. The matter being raised, you would say, "Well, I think in the range of $36,000 to $40,000 would be fair."

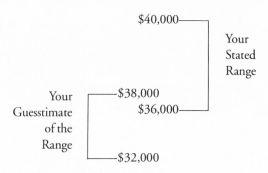

Crystal's emphasis is that your researched value should be built on a foundation of solid fact. When it is, you'll get credit for frankness, savvy, and thoroughness, by being able to lay out your dollar facts at any time.

To evaluate this strategy, it's crucial to understand that it is done within the context of Crystal's unique job-hunting methods. For the most part, *Crystals' followers are creating brand new positions.* They're coming to management with a proposal for a job instead of applying for openings someone else has defined. *So the prospective employers may not know what the proposed position is worth.* In that case you'll be helping out by offering a suggestion that makes good business sense. And since there is no one applying for the position but you, there is no reason to worry that by revealing your price you will be underbid by competitors for the job. Therefore it could be an exception in those circumstances for you to discuss compensation first or while your proposal is being considered prior to the offer. It could be a way of educating them about the value of the job proposal.

On the other hand, unearthing the actual salaries of your prospective employers is tough, and you still run the risk of getting rejected while the hirer is in the **budget** stage. In addition, you run the risk of losing an offer because your research was incorrect, and your figure didn't make good bottom-line business sense. When *they* go first, you have an offer. When *you* go first, you don't.

So I'd recommend, even when negotiating an offer for a created-just-for-you position, that you postpone compensation talk until your employer-to-be really wants to buy. "You may be wondering how much I'll cost you," you say, "and that's a legitimate concern. But I won't cost you a nickel unless my proposal makes sense, and then I intend to make you money, not cost you money—so let's make sure this proposal will work." Then have them come up with a first guess of its value—you counter with your research.

"What If They Get Mad at Me?"

People sometimes excuse themselves from following salary-making rule 1 by saying, "If I don't answer the salary question, the interviewer will get mad at me, and I'll *never* get the job!" Indeed, some interviewers declare a staunch inflexibility about their budget right away, like:

"This position pays $_____; there's no negotiating. If that's not acceptable to you, then let's end the interview now."

"I absolutely have to know your current earnings."

"This application must be filled out *completely* before the interview can proceed."

They may feel frustrated that they can't screen you; sometimes you'll notice that your interviewer seems perturbed, thinks you're not being cooperative. You worry that this will get in the way of building the rapport essential to being hired.

First, let me say that this is the exception. Following the guidelines in Chapters 3 and 4, you will find most interviewers quite amenable to postponing salary talk once they're reassured that you'll accept a fair salary. Second, odds are that they're worried you're too expensive (people rarely get upset about you being too cheap). As long as *you* know that you're interviewing at the right level, or that there's *potential* to reach the right level of responsibility, it's to your advantage that they wonder about affording you!

So, if you're tempted to go first, to discuss price before value just to placate the interviewer, think twice; and also, when you do find yourself in that tension in an interview, remember that your old habits will steer you to the path of least resistance. I'll discuss how *you* can control your habits in the next chapter. For now, if your habits are controlling you, you will feel like going first. Here are three ways to handle that impulse: least effective (and easiest), better, and best.

Least Effective: The least effective way is to cave in, and reveal your salary history or requirements. You risk losing several thousand dollars in that twenty-second conversation, and you risk being screened out as

97

too cheap or too expensive. Coughing up a salary figure will get you off the hook, but since it compromises the principles of being hired on value not price, it's not a tremendously positive sign for starting a virtuous cycle.

If, however, you *do* choose this least effective method, at *least* discuss your salary *expectations*, not your *history*. Determine your market value (see Chapter 5) and communicate a range: "Well, I expect a fair salary for this kind of position. My research indicates a range of $X to $Y, but every job is unique, so let's discuss the job and my potential in it. Then we'll both have a better idea of my value."

Better: If you choose to bypass salary-making rule 1 (wait for an offer), there's still a chance to follow salary-making rule 2 (they go first). When they're adamant about discussing salary, you can probe their budget, and tell them that it's a good starting point. For example, "My salary expectations? They're simple: a fair market value. Perhaps you could help me there; what is the range you're thinking of? I'd be glad to tell you if it fits."

When they tell you their range, say, "That's in the right ballpark; I'm sure we can make a good salary agreement if you want to hire me. Let's keep talking."

Best: Stick to your principles. You don't have to answer every single question an interviewer asks; you're not on the witness stand. Often you can defuse discomfort by commenting on it, like: "I find talking about money at this point awkward; perhaps you do too? I hope I am not upsetting you by asking to postpone it."

You can finish up with some of the responses at the end of Chapter 4. Nancy's response works well. Or something like, "You see, I know this is the kind of work, and the level of responsibility that I want. If I'm valuable to you, I'm sure that finding a fair salary will take care of itself."

This "best" kind of response takes practice. Most people have interviewing habits, and most often they have the specific one of answering every question they're asked *as if the interviewer really knows what to ask!* I have news for you. Interviewers act out of habit, too!

In the final chapter, let's take a look at our habits and their impact on salary negotiations.

CHAPTER ELEVEN

Practice & Coaching

Changing Habits Through Practice

This book has supplied the logic, scripts, and strategy tools that you'll need to change your habits about salary talk. But that's not enough. Even if you commit this entire book to memory, when you show up at Mr. Employer's office you'll probably slip back into the same old ways. Unless you practice.

Most of us are not used to negotiating for ourselves. Our present habits push us to do just the opposite: accept what's offered and hope for the best. To understand how to break habits, let's find out how entrenched they tend to be. It's important to recognize that these habits are comfortable and help us run our lives smoothly.

Think of all the habits you live out in the first half hour of each day. Turning off the alarm? Pressing the "snooze" button? Do you find the toothpaste, toothbrush, and hair dryer in the same place every time? If you had to think about each step, and search for the soap and cereal every morning, it would take twice as long *and* not get done as well. For example, you can probably remember the hours it took you to do routine chores when you last moved into a new home and had to establish new habits.

Now let's try an experiment. Put this book down, fold your hands, and notice which "pinky" finger is on the bottom. Now, refold your hands with the *other* pinky finger on the bottom. How does it feel?

☐ comfortable   ☐ uncomfortable

Uncomfortable, naturally!

Which way is correct? Neither, of course. Your way is just your habit; the other way is just the uncomfortable way. It makes no difference which way you fold your hands, and yet you'll do it the same comfortable way every single time!

Here's a more challenging experiment: Try folding your arms. Notice whether the left arm or the right arm is on top. Go ahead!

Now, see how many times it takes you to fold them so that the *other* arm is on top. Please do it until you can "reverse fold" them, at will. If you can do it *with ease* in less than ten tries, you're terrific.

Salary and raise negotiations, needless to say, are much more complicated than folding your arms. Poor habits about salary talk will take practice to change. You can practice alone by writing a script, using a tape recorder, or talking to a mirror. An even faster way to change them is through practice *and coaching*.

Practice and Coaching Is Even Better

Coaching helps us see ourselves objectively. That's why tennis lessons from a coach will correct in one hour what someone may have tried to correct by themselves for weeks. The same goes for baseball, football, golf, hockey, aerobics, and jogging. It's true for negotiations, too. Someone with ears *other than your own* can give you objective feedback that will help you handle yourself better. Use friends, counselors, or telephone sessions.

A friend or acquaintance can help you by role-playing. Have them ask you the tricky questions; it will probably help to have them read Chapter 3 so they get into the employer's frame of mind about screening.

Professional career consultants are another excellent resource. In my work, coaching salary negotiations is only one of the hundreds of coaching areas in a total career management program. Some career counselors are available on a per session basis. I believe that *any* investment of time and money with a good "career coach" will probably pay for itself several times over. This is dramatically true about a salary negotiations consultation. (Sometimes they've been worth as much as $1,000 a minute!) For a list of career counseling resources, check:

What Color Is Your Parachute? by Richard N. Bolles. Ten Speed Press, Berkeley, CA. Parachute's Appendix C is a list of career-counseling resources across the country, updated yearly.

College placement offices may have some experienced counselors, too, although they more often specialize in academic vocational choice counseling. So, take care to check out the actual experience of your potential counselor. Good coaching is worth paying for; poor coaching will cost you money.

Telecoaching Service

Readers have called me many times since this book was first published. I have enjoyed these calls. You, too, are welcome to consult with me and my staff by phone if you wish.

Here are a few stories to give you a flavor of what we can get done through telecoaching. I've picked some of the more interesting ones because I think you'll enjoy reading them and because you will see a few twists and turns in applying the five salary making rules in these examples.

Public Relations Professional

Situation: George called about a salaried public relations position in a hospital. The hospital was losing money. In the midst of cutbacks and salary freezes, George didn't know how to get a raise. "I'll just be happy to keep my job," he said.

Telecoaching: In reviewing his boss's goals, however, we found that the addictions treatment center was profitable and the one area on which the boss pinned his hopes for growth.

George and I spotted the boss's hot button, identified a few of George's P.R. accomplishments especially as they related to the center, and we developed an outline of a P.R. campaign to build the center's visibility and credibility. While George was not able to get an immediate salary increase, he did negotiate a bonus based on the overall use of the center which we estimated could net $2,000-$4,000 a year.

Management Consultant

Situation: A high level international business consultant was interviewing for an operations management position with a nationwide food distributor. The recruiter told Frank that $115,000 was the top that the company would go.

Telecoaching: We were able to find (or find out how to find) three "navigation points" to guide us: a cost of living index, comparable salaries, and a specific trouble spot Frank could handle with dispatch that could save the company $50,000 annually. He arranged to negotiate directly with the hiring decision makers and made his case. Frank got $20,000 more plus a performance bonus up to 50 percent of his salary.

Product Manager for High Tech Marketing Product

Situation : Virginia's stumper was how to negotiate a lateral transfer where she thought (but wasn't sure) she was already making more than her prospective new boss.

Telecoaching: We worked out a way to present the dilemma to personnel that allowed them to give Virginia her parameters without actually revealing her boss's earnings. We also strategized a way her new boss might get a raise.

She changed positions, kept her salary, and in the first month she taught her boss how to negotiate a better deal for himself as well as for Virginia. Now they're both earning more than when they began.

Village Engineer

Situation : Jim was hired by a small village to be the village engineer. He felt the offer was low, but the village manager couldn't go outside the budget, and the budget couldn't be changed until the new village board reviewed it in the fall.

Telecoaching: To get around it, however, Jim asked for and got a relocation package (tax free) that was not in the original offer. This boosted his earnings and tided him over until the regular salary review process could make his earnings more competitive.

Of course, we also set up a plan to make sure the manager *and* the new board would be very well informed of his value by the time the fall budget review would take place.

Marketing Manager/Sales Manager

Situation : Dave originally interviewed for a position for which he was overqualified. During the interview the sales V.P. & operations manager were impressed with Dave, and called the President in to discuss upgrading the position. They did; but just as a camel is humorously called "a horse designed by a committee," this new position was pasted together with two conflicting sets of responsibilities. As it stood, the job was 50-percent sales, sales support, and on-site troubleshooting, and 50-percent strategic planning. This combination had conflicting elements which would doom it to failure. Dave wanted 10-percent sales and 90-percent planning; he was also pushing for $20,000 more now, and even more interesting money later. He also knew that two of the three people in on the decision would fight energetically to keep the 50-percent sales/sales support.

Telecoaching: First Dave needed coaching on how to avoid premature salary discussions. Even though they were technically making him an offer, they hadn't really decided for which job. In our discussion it became clear that he was not on salary-making rule 2 (they go first), but rather rule 1 which, in Dave's case, would be "Postpone salary talk until they know which job they want to offer."

The strategy we worked out was to concentrate on a five-year plan rather than on a present position opening. By submitting a two-page outline of such a plan, Dave was able to pull the attention of all three decision makers to the big picture. He also offered an alternative way to get the 50 percent all done. Dave spent a total of twenty minutes delaying, and later discussing compensation, and he increased the salary $20,000 ($1,000 a minute), and negotiated a profit-sharing bonus based on his five-year performance plan.

Computer Specialist

Situation: Similarly, I told Jerry to break the rules. Usually the base salary is handled first, then the bennies and perks. However, Jerry knew he would want certain pieces of computer hardware to get the results the employer wanted on the job.

Telecoaching: I coached him to say, "Salary and benefits are important Mr. Employer, but having the tools to do the job for you is my first concern. Let's discuss the computer investment I want you to make and if we can agree on that, I'm sure compensation will be no problem."

When negotiating this "perk," Jerry's attitude was "Even if you offered me a huge salary, I would have to say no if the tools don't come with it." The employer was impressed with his integrity and commitment to results. Jerry got the hardware, *and* a better compensation package to boot.

Direct Mail Marketer

Situation: Amy had a huge opportunity to make money on the back end. She was not aware of it and called only to practice her normal negotiation pitch.

Telecoaching: We practiced the regular rules to bring her salary up 10 percent. Then I showed her this back-end gold mine. We rehearsed negotiating for bennies on each renewal transaction from original accounts she generated *if and only if* the accounts were profitable from *her* copywriting. Each year thereafter her earnings jumped $10-$15,000.

City Manager

Situation: A city manager had a poor performance review and therefore a small raise.

Telecoaching: It took us two half-hour sessions to work up a strategy because there were seven city commissioners and three would change in three months. By rigorous questioning and evaluating, he discovered the real "hot buttons" for each commissioner. The manager realized he would need some special management training and personal development courses if he was ever going to meet their expectations. By proposing a specific, eighteen-step plan for self improvement and better performance, he saved his job. (He found out later that the small raise was a first step in a push to get him to quit. The commissioners had actually been planning to terminate him.) He is now well on his way to recouping all his lost-salary ground the next time.

The above examples were somewhat complicated; most people's telecoaching needs are much simpler. Often in telecoaching you'll just confirm and solidify a straightforward application of the five salary-making rules. Sometimes its main benefit is to give needed encouragement and practice.

On Getting the Courage to Negotiate

"I couldn't believe I said what I did." J.G. (Clerk)

"I kept hearing your voice during the interview and I said those magic words. . . . I think *I* was more surprised at my chutzpah than my boss was. It helped and it worked." T.S. (Manufacturer's Rep)

"If you hadn't bawled me out for being wimpy, I'd have given up. I'm still a wimp, overall, but at least I'm earning more money!" L.W. (Customer Service Rep)

"One needs one's spirit pumped up, so to speak, to really stand up for what one deserves. Thanks." M.C. (Educator)

"Hearing you say 'You can do it' made me feel that I could do it. . . . I did it!" M.B. (Events Planner)

". . . He then said, 'Equity?! You want Equity too?!' I thought I went too far, but I got it, and he was impressed." B.T. (Music Company Manager)

"At first I thought, 'This is preposterous! I have no right to ask for all that . . . after [our telecoaching] I saw how I really had been cheating *myself*. It wasn't my boss's fault, it was me believing that I should really get . . . what I deserve. When I finally asked for it, it seemed like the most reasonable thing on earth." (Accountant)

On Practice

"I kept wanting you to go and talk for me. You had so many great ways to say things. When I finally did it, though, they weren't *your* words anymore. I had used your words enough to make them my own." K.B. (Nurse)

"Practice makes perfect . . . but for me practice with you made it possible." R.D.M. (Counselor)

"I thought I knew how to do this. I read the book a hundred times! But it was different saying it out loud somehow. Anyway it worked, thanks." W.B.C. (Engineer)

"Somebody should make everybody rehearse their lines about salary negotiations. Rehearsing answers to every possible response is what made my $5,000 happen." J.W. (Salesman)

"I never could have stated my case like that if we hadn't practiced . . . I tell my friends that I argued my case with a lawyer and I won!" M.L. (Legal Secretary)

Arranging Personal Telecoaching

If you'd like to strategize, rehearse, or just review what you've been thinking, you are welcome to set up a telecoaching session. Here's what to do. Call me at (312) 346-5835 and set an appointment time. My assistant will schedule the time (generally a half-hour is enough) and hold it with a credit card. You can mail (FAX) me material in advance if you think it will help. At the appointed time, you'll call me and we'll have a good go at it.

Caution: don't get into an either/or trap here: *either* telecoaching with me *or* practicing with friends. Do both! I encourage you to practice with others in addition to whatever telecoaching you might arrange.

Your Goal in All This

I strongly urge you to practice. Find a friend or coach who will role-play the employer. Have them probe for your present salary and your expectations. Get them to finally extend an offer—you counter with your researched response. Consult Chapters 3 and 4; write out or make up responses that feel right to you. Rehearse them. Tape record a couple of sessions if you wish. The goal is to *make it comfortable.*

While negotiating may never be 100-percent comfortable for you, you can still make it sound more and more natural. Many of my clients tell me how, after practicing, their money-talk flows smoothly and effortlessly. They *habitually* follow the key principle: Value First, Price Second.

The practice you put in will generate new, good habits and a high level of comfort, *and* the employer will interpret that comfort level as confidence which will help your negotiations be even more successful!

POSTSCRIPT

Good luck!

I hope reading this book helps you take your salary seriously. When compensation is negotiated in a win/win way, both you and your employer will be motivated to get the very best performance and accomplishment from the situation. This, in turn, will produce more money for the employer and career satisfaction and success for you.

May you always be part of the virtuous cycle: achievement . . . good pay . . . more achievement . . . better pay . . . even more achievement . . .

Excerpt and Charts from National Salary Survey

The "Compendium of Salary Research Sources and Methods" section in Chapter 5 noted that the *National Survey of Professional, Administrative, Technical, and Clerical Pay,* issued each year by the U.S. Department of Labor Statistics, is one of the most accessible tools for discovering what price your skills can command in the job market. That information helps prepare you to negotiate for top dollar.

One problem the survey can help you with is judging the level of responsibility that your prospective job involves. For example, "systems analyst" for the Apple IIe at Fred's Bar & Grill is several steps below "systems analyst" for GM's new interplant production and inventory control system. In order to research what your salary should be, you need to be able to describe clearly what your responsibilities would be.

The survey is also very useful as an example of how to categorize your target job's level of responsibility.

I've chosen to present the "Secretary" section of the survey because I believe all employees can grasp its principles of categorization and then apply them to their own target jobs.

The excerpt is from the 1985 survey.

Secretary

Provides principal secretarial support in an office, usually to one individual, and, in some cases, to the subordinate staff of that individual as well. Maintains a close and highly responsive relationship to the day-to-day activities of the supervisor and staff. Works fairly independently, receiving a minimum of detailed supervision and guidance. Performs varied clerical and secretarial duties requiring a knowledge of office routine and an understanding of the organization, programs, and procedures related to the work of the office.

Table C-5. Criteria for matching secretaries by level.

Level of Secretary's Supervisor	Level of Secretary's Responsibility			
	LR-1	LR-2	LR-3	LR-4
	Level of Position as It Relates to Salary			
LS 1	I	II	III	IV
LS 2	I	III	IV	V
LS 3	I	IV	V	V

Exclusions. Not all positions titled "secretary" possess the above characteristics. Examples of positions which are excluded from the definition are as follows.

(a) Clerks or secretaries working under the direction of secretaries or administrative assistants as described in (e);

(b) Stenographers not fully performing secretarial duties;

(c) Stenographers or secretaries assigned to two or more professional, technical, or managerial persons of equivalent rank;

(d) Assistants or secretaries performing any kind of technical work, e.g., personnel, accounting, or legal work;

(e) Administrative assistants or supervisors performing duties which are more difficult or more responsible than the secretarial work described in LR-1 through LR-4 (pages 112 - 115);

(f) Secretaries receiving additional pay primarily for maintaining confidentiality of payroll records or other sensitive information;

(g) Secretaries performing routine receptionist, typing, and filing duties following detailed instructions and guidelines; these duties are less responsible than those described in LR-1 (page 112);

(h) Trainees.

Classification by Level

Secretary jobs which meet the required characteristics are matched at one of five levels according to two factors: (a) level of the secretary's supervisor within the overall organizational structure, and (b) level of the secretary's responsibility. Table C-5 on the preceding page indicates the level of the secretary for each combination of factors.

LEVEL OF SECRETARY'S SUPERVISORS (LS)

Secretaries should be matched at one of the three LS levels which best describe the organization of the secretary's supervisor.

LS-2. Organizational structure is complex and is divided into subordinate groups that usually differ from each other as to subject matter, function, etc.; supervisor usually directs staff through intermediate supervisors; internal procedures and administrative controls are formal. An entire organization (e.g., division, subsidiary, or parent organization) may contain a variety of subordinate groups which meet the LS-2 definition. Therefore, it is not unusual for one LS-2 supervisor to report to another LS-2 supervisor.

The presence of subordinate supervisors does not by itself mean LS-2 applies, e.g., a clerical processing organization divided into several units, each performing very similar work, is placed in LS-1.

In smaller organizations or industries such as retail trade, with relatively few organizational levels, the supervisor may have an impact on the policies and may deal with important outside contracts, as described in LS-3.

LS-3. Organizational structure is divided into two or more subordinate supervisory levels (of which at least one is a managerial level) with several subdivisions at each level. Executive's program(s) are usually interlocked on a direct and continuing basis with other major organizational segments, requiring constant attention to extensive formal coordination, clearances, and procedural controls. Executive typically has: financial decision-making authority for assigned program(s); considerable impact on the entire organization's financial position or image; and responsibility for, or has staff specialists in, such areas as personnel and administration for assigned organization. Executives play an important role in determining the policies and major programs of the entire organization, and spend considerable time dealing with outside parties actively interested in assigned program(s) and current or controversial issues.

LEVEL OF SECRETARY'S RESPONSIBILITY (LR)

This factor evaluates the nature of the work relationship between the secretary and the supervisor or staff, and the extent to which the secretary is expected to exercise initiative and judgment. Secretaries should be matched at the level best describing their level of responsibility. When a position's duties span more than one LR level, the introductory paragraph at the beginning of each LR level should be used to determine which of the levels best matches the position. (Typically, secretaries performing at the higher levels of responsibility also perform duties described at the lower levels.)

LR-1. Carries out recurring office procedures independently. Selects the guideline or reference which fits the specific case. Supervisor provides specific instructions on new assignments and checks completed work for accuracy. Performs varied duties including or comparable to the following:

(a) Responds to routine telephone requests which have standard answers; refers calls and visitors to appropriate staff. Controls mail and assures timely staff response; may send form letters.

(b) As instructed, maintains supervisor's calendar, makes appointments, and arranges for meeting rooms.

(c) Reviews materials prepared for supervisor's approval for typographical accuracy and proper format.

(d) Maintains recurring internal reports, such as: Time and leave records, office equipment listings, correspondence controls, training plans, etc.

(e) Requisitions supplies, printing, maintenance, or other services. Types, takes and transcribes dictation, and establishes and maintains office files.

112

LR-2. Handles differing situations, problems, and deviations in the work of the office according to the supervisor's general instructions, priorities, duties, policies, and program goals. Supervisor may assist secretary with special assignments. Duties include or are comparable to the following:

(a) Screens telephone calls, visitors, and incoming correspondence; personally responds to requests for information concerning office procedures; determines which requests should be handled by the supervisor, appropriate staff members, or other offices. May prepare and sign routine, nontechnical correspondence in own or supervisor's name.

(b) Schedules tentative appointments without prior clearance. Makes arrangements for conferences and meetings and assembles established background materials, as directed. May attend meetings and record and report on the proceedings.

(c) Reviews outgoing materials and correspondence for internal consistency and conformance with supervisor's procedures; assures that proper clearances have been obtained, when needed.

(d) Collects information from the files or staff for routine inquiries on office program(s) or periodic reports. Refers nonroutine requests to supervisor or staff.

(e) Explains to subordinate staff supervisor's requirements concerning office procedures. Coordinates personnel and administrative forms for the office and forwards for processing.

LR-3. Uses greater judgment and initiative to determine the approach or action to take in nonroutine situations. Interprets and adapts guidelines, including unwritten policies, precedents, and practices, which are not always completely applicable to changing situations. Duties include or are comparable to the following:

(a) Based on a knowledge of the supervisor's views, composes correspondence on own initiative about administrative and general office policies for supervisor's approval.

(b) Anticipates and prepares materials needed by the supervisor for conferences, correspondence, appointments, meetings, telephone calls, etc., and informs supervisor on matters to be considered.

(c) Reads publications, regulations, and directives and takes action or refers those that are important to the supervisor and staff.

(d) Prepares special or one-time reports, summaries, or replies to inquiries, selecting relevant information from a variety of sources such as reports, documents, correspondence, other offices, etc., under general direction.

(e) Advises secretaries in subordinate offices on new procedures; requests information needed from the subordinate office(s) for periodic or special conferences, reports, inquiries, etc. Shifts clerical staff to accommodate workload needs.

LR-4. Handles a wide variety of situations and conflicts involving the clerical or administrative functions of the office which often cannot be brought to the attention of the executive. The executive sets the overall objectives of the work. Secretary may participate in developing the work deadlines. Duties include or are comparable to the following:

(a) Composes correspondence requiring some understanding of technical matters; may sign for executive when technical or policy content has been authorized.

(b) Notes commitments made by executive during meetings and arranges for staff implementation. On own initiative, arranges for staff member to represent organization at conferences and meetings; establishes appointment priorities, or reschedules or refuses appointments or invitations.

(c) Reads outgoing correspondence for executive's approval and alerts writers to any conflict with the file or departure from policies or executive's viewpoints; gives advice to resolve the problems.

(d) Summarizes the content of incoming materials, especially gathered information, or meetings to assist executive; coordinates the new information with background office sources; and draws attention to important parts or conflicts.

(e) In the executive's absence ensures that requests for action or information are relayed to the appropriate staff member; as needed, interprets request and helps implement action; makes sure that information is furnished in timely manner; decides whether executives should be notified of important or emergency matters.

This category excludes secretaries performing any of the following duties:

(a) Acts as office manager for the executive's organization, e.g., determines when new procedures are needed for changing situations and devises and implements alternatives; revises or clarifies procedures to eliminate conflict or duplication; identifies and resolves various problems that affect the orderly flow of work in transactions with parties outside the organization.

(b) Prepares agenda for conferences; explains discussion topics to participants; drafts introductions, develops background information, and prepares outlines for executive or staff member(s) to use in writing speeches.

(c) Advises individuals outside the organization on the executive's views on major policies or current issues facing the organization; contacts or responds to contacts from high-ranking outside officials (e.g., city or state officials, members of Congress, presidents of national unions, or large national or international firms, etc.) in unique situations. These officials may be relatively inaccessible, and each contact typically must be handled differently, using judgment and discretion.

ABOUT THE AUTHOR

Jack Chapman is President of the Chicago office of Bernard Haldane Associates, a career development consulting firm. He is the cofounder and past president of the Professional Career Counselors and Consultants Network (PCCN). As a career consultant, Jack has helped people from every walk of life land exactly the jobs, salaries, and raises they've wanted.

Following his undergraduate studies at Loyola University, Jack earned his master's in vocational guidance at Northeastern Illinois University. He taught on the faculty of Chicago's Columbia College, where he pioneered a career development curriculum. His seminars include "A Streetwise Guide to Job Interviewing," "Career Development for Women," "Beyond the Help Wanted Ads," "How to Put an Extra Grand in your Paycheck," and "Golden Complaints: 'If Only . . .' Opportunities in Your Job."

Jack has appeared on network television representing career counselors, delivered numerous speeches and lectures, and conducted countless workshops and seminars.

He lives in Wilmette, a suburb of Chicago, with his wife and three children.